CHRISTIAN, NON-CHRISTIAN DIALOGUE:

The Vision of Robert C. Zaehner

Richard L. Schebera

University Press
of America™

Library of Congress Catalog Card Number: 78-64369

TABLE OF CONTENTS

INTRODUCTION

Since this study deals largely with the thought of Professor Zaehner it will be well to give at the outset some biographical information. Born in 1913, he benefitted from fine education and soon distinguished himself as a serious student. He studied at both Cambridge and Oxford Universities in England, and it was at Oxford that he was Senior Scholar of Christ Church from 1937-1939, as well as Research Lecturer of Christ Church in 1939. It was also at Oxford that he gained a Master's degree in Oriental languages, and where he lectured in Persian in 1950. This linguistic interest was a characteristic throughout his scholarly career.

Zaehner served as press attaché for the British Embassy in Teheran from 1943-1947 and acting counsellor from 1951-1952. It was during this latter period of his life that he returned to Oxford as a lecturer, and also began to publish his first serious studies on Zoroastrianism. In 1952 he was chosen as Spalding Professor of Eastern Religions and Ethics, All Souls College, Oxford, a position which he held until his death in 1974. It was also at this time that he began serious studies in Hinduism and Buddhism, and especially, as a linguist, in Sanskrit. During these years he became a respected name in the field of Comparative Religion, as well as an international lecturer. The bibliography at the end of this work indicates the number of times that he was chosen as a major lecturer. His works are also listed chronologically to show the development of his thought, and to indicate that his latest works were especially in the Theology of Religion.

Zaehner distinguished himself, first of all, as a linguist by translations and detailed textual work. Most of this work was in Persian and Sanskrit, and it was for Zaehner a necessary approach to religious understanding. He felt that without an understanding of the scripture of a religion one could not understand that religion. Secondly, Zaehner equipped himself with a theological

1

understanding of the religions that he treated.
Although he frequently discussed various religions
in their relationship to Christianity, still he
tried to understand various religions in themselves
and as they are understood by their own theologians.
Whether he was totally successful in this understanding is a moot point. Some of his interpretations
are debatable and objectionable to other scholars.
This is expected in scholarly research. The
strength of some of Zaehner's arguments are as
strong as the validity of his interpretations of
the religions involved.

Because of this combination of skills Zaehner
was considered as one of the best qualified scholars
in England to speak on the subject of Comparative
Religion. In addition, he had an international
reputation in this field. Although some of his recent books are more commentaries on the religious
scene rather than serious theological efforts, this
may have resulted from the uncharted path that religious dialogue is to take, or to the visionary
efforts which Zaehner intended.

Perhaps one of the most interesting aspects
of studying Zaehner's writings is that he is representative of a large segment of Christian thinking
on the subject of Christianity and the non-Christian
religions. Zaehner's presentation of Christianity
as the fulfillment of the religious aspirations of
other religions is typical of the positions of many
other Christian thinkers. Thus, a study of Zaehner
is a study of a much larger segment of Christianity.

The relationship between Christianity and
the other religions of the world is the task to
which Zaehner set himself. What judgment does a
Christian make concerning other religions? What is
the role of Christ and the Church in relation to
other religions? On what basis can tolerant dialogue
exist between the Christian and the non-Christian?
These are the kinds of questions to which Zaehner
addressed himself in his writings. The answer that
he has found is that Christ is ultimately the fulfillment of the religious aspirations of mankind as
well as the coherent pattern to religious history.
This conclusion did not result, said Zaehner, from
the fact that after a period of his life without
any religious belief he became a convert to Catholicism. He claimed that he was not an apologist for

his particular religious tradition. Rather, this
emphasis on the centrality of Christ was the result
of his scholarship, and the way he had come to see
things. He presented his convictions and scholarship not only for Catholics, nor only for Christians,
but for all people who are interested in the dialogue
among the religions of the world.

In seeing how Zaehner came to his conclusions
we shall, first of all, study his methodology. After
this we shall examine his Christology, his Ecclesiology, and his view of Mysticism, as they relate to
other world religions. In the final chapter we shall
evaluate Zaehner's work, especially his Christology
and Ecclesiology. Since his argumentation for Christian mysticism is based on the fulfillment model this
will be considered under the general evaluation of
the fulfillment model in itself.

The concluding chapter will evaluate both the
strengths and weaknesses of Zaehner's insight into
Christ and the Church as fulfillments of the religious aspirations of other religions. It will
evaluate these points in their usefulness for the
Christian and their possible use in present day
inter-religious dialogue. Since the fulfillment
model presents some serious difficulties for this
dialogue, some alternate proposals have been indicated. The proposals will perhaps be a better means
of self-understanding for the Christian as he
approaches people of other faiths. They may also be
a better basis for realistic dialogue.

CHAPTER I

A CRITICAL UNDERSTANDING OF ZAEHNER'S

METHODOLOGY OF DIALOGUE

The Choice Between a Phenomenology or a Theology of Religions

In order to understand Professor Zaehner's attitude towards the dialogue between world religions, some introductory remarks concerning methodology are in order. There are many possible ways of approaching the dialogue between major world religions. That a plurality of ways exists indicates the complexity of the task. Attempts at understanding in this field require nuanced thought and precise presentation. Failure to do so can only result in generalizations and misrepresentations.

For this reason we will distinguish briefly in the following pages between a phenomenology and a theology of religions. This will be done to show the background to Zaehner's method of inter-religious dialogue. It will also help us to determine what Zaehner's method is, as well as its justification. There are times when he works as an exegete of world scriptures, other times as a phenomenologist, and other times, especially as we will see in chapters two, three, and four, as a theologian of religions. The latter method is a legitimate one, and if we understand it from the beginning we can forestall objections of bias or triumphalism.

The phenomenological[1] approach to religion

---

[1]It is difficult to determine what constitutes Phenomenology of Religion. C. F. George Widengren, "An Introduction to the Phenomenology of Religion," in Ways of Understanding Religion, ed. W. Capps (New York: Macmillan, 1972), pp. 142-51. Also C. J. Bleeker, "The Entelecheia of Religious

is an effort to understand religion according to its own inner meaning. In commenting on the respected scholar W. B. Kristensen's definition of the phenomenology of religion, Heindrik Kraemer notes that it is

> the systematically pursued, comparative endeavour to interpret and understand religious phenomena of the same category (sacrifice, prayer, sacraments, etc.) appearing in different religions, to get at their inner meaning. The requirement, he says, is a scrupulous reverence for the facts and genuinely sympathetic understanding. It is for the true phenomenologist the lifelong education in the right art of empathy for the subject of his research. . . . The Phenomenologist's task is to enter into the mind of the believer. To understand a religious phenomenon as the believer understands or understood it, is the true job of the phenomenologist. . . . This understanding is, according to Kristensen, quite different from attaining to the faith of the believer.[2]

Phenomena," The Sacred Bridge (Leiden: E. J. Brill, pp. 16-24. The Phenomenology of Religion can be distinguished from the History of Religion cf. Widengren, p. 142, or can be distinguished from Comparative Religion cf. W. C. Smith, "On the Comparative Study of Religion," McGill University Divinity Faculty Inaugural Lectures (Montreal: The University Press, 1950), pp. 39-60. Nevertheless, there are times when Comparative Religion, History of Religion, and Scientific Study of Religion are used in almost the same sense as Phenomenology of Religion, i.e., all are concerned with the 'objective' approach of 'Religionswissenschaft.' Cf. R. D. Baird, Category Formation and the History of Religions (The Hague: Mouton, 1971), and also J. M. Kitagawa, "The History of Religious Subjectivity," in The History of Religions: Essays in Methodology, ed. Mircea Eliade (Chicago: University of Chicago Press, 1959), pp. 28ff.

[2] W. B. Kristensen, The Meaning of Religion: Lectures in the Phenomenology of Religion, from the Foreword by Heindrik Kraemer (The Hague: Martinus Nijhoff, 1960), pp. xxi-xxii.

Phenomenology does not try to compare the religions with one another as large units, but it takes out of their historical setting the similar facts and phenomena which it encounters in different religions, brings them together, and studies them in groups. The corresponding data, which are sometimes nearly identical, bring us almost automatically to comparative study. The purpose of such study is to become acquainted with the religious thought, idea or need which underlies the group of corresponding data. Its purpose is not to determine their greater or lesser religious value. Certainly, it tries to determine their religious value, but this is the value that they have had for the believers themselves. Phenomenology tries to gain an over-all view of the ideas and motives which are of decisive importance in the History of Religions.

We call this kind of study phenomenological because it is concerned with the systematic treatment of phenomena. Phenomenology is a systematic science, not just a historical discipline which considers the Greek, Roman or Egyptian religion by itself. The problem is to determine what sacrifice itself is, not just what Greek, Roman, or Hebrew sacrifice is. It is clear that Phenomenology in this way makes an important contribution towards a better and deeper understanding of the separate historical data.[3]

C. J. Bleeker sees this understanding in terms of objectives which he calls the theoria and the logos of the phenomena. The theoria of the phenomena leads to an understanding of the religious implications of various aspects of religion which occur all over the world, such as sacrifice, prayer and the magic arts. The logos of the phenomena uncovers the hidden structure of the different religions by showing that they are built up according to strict inner laws.[4]

He goes on to mention that the Phenomenology of religion comprises two principles, namely the epoché and the eidetic vision. The first principle means the suspension of judgment. In using the

---

[3]Ibid., pp. 3-4.

[4]Bleeker, "The Phenomenological Method," p.14.

epoché one puts oneself into the position of the
listener, who does not judge according to precon-
ceived notions. Applied to the phenomenology of
religion, this means that this science cannot concern itself with the question of the truth of
religion. Phenomenology must begin by accepting as
proper objects of study all phenomena that are pro-
fessed to be religious. Subsequently the attempt
may come to distinguish what is genuinely religious
from what is spurious. The second principle, that
of the eidetic vision, can easily be understood. It
has as its aim the search of the eidos, that is the
essentials of religious phenomena.[5]

What has been said thus far should convince
us that the scientific study of religion excludes in
principle judgments of value and truth. Such judgments lead us into another category viz. the theology
of religions because it would no longer compare e.g.
historical matter with historical matter, but
historical matter with a believer's theological interpretation of history.

It is therefore a misunderstanding to assert
that the phenomenology of religion passes, in any
sense, a judgment on the question of the truth of
religion. It only maintains its position of impartiality by demanding that all religion should be
understood as what it stands for, namely as a serious
testimony of religious people that they possess a
knowledge of God. That means that it on the one side
rejects the idea that there should be only one true
religion, and on the other hand debates the contention that there is no true religion, as though all
religion could be reduced to human psychological or
social factors.[6]

The phenomenology of religion then, does not
concern the question of the comparative values of
different religions, nor the truth of different
religions. On the other hand, the theology of religions does deal with these questions. And, as we
shall see, Zaehner deals almost exclusively in this
theological questioning. It is almost a necessity,
in his view, to go beyond the phenomenological level
to the theological level, for it is natural for one
to compare to judge and to evaluate. The result of
such activity is a deeper understanding of religions

---

[5]Ibid., p. 3.   [6]Ibid., p. 9.

8

and their claims. Such is the way Zaehner understands his theological work of comparing religions.

> I concern myself with the great religions and
> ethical systems of the East, the setting forth
> of their development and spiritual meaning, and
> the interpretation of them by comparison and
> contrast with each other and with the religions
> and ethics of the West. This is what I under-
> stand by Comparative Religion or, to be more
> precise, the comparative study of religion.[7]

One can also ask whether the presupposition
of phenomenology of religion, that experience is
basic to the question of truth, leaves sufficient
room for revelation. Thus, Heindrik Kraemer who
has been associated with a conservative wing of the
theology of religions writes:

> With Kristensen's exclusive stress on the full
> right of the diverse religious intuitions, he
> is involuntarily driven towards a blurring of
> the majestic problem of Truth, which lies behind
> the undeniable reality of experience and value.
> . . . I always defended the ultimate rightness
> of a theological approach, based on a different
> concerption of the relation of truth and ex-
> perience. Kristensen accepted the absolutely
> basic character of experience in formulating
> the problem of Truth. For me, on the other hand,
> experience as a chief element in the problem of
> Truth, is truly relevant, but not basic.[8]

In fact, the very possibility of detached
religio-historical knowledge has been thrown into
question by Heindrik Kraemer. His contention is that
the claim of religio-historical knowledge to be
"scientific" and "objective" is nothing more than a
claim. The goal of understanding cannot be achieved
without interpretation. Value-judgments inevitably
enter into the study, which is to say that the

---

[7]R. G. Zaehner, At Sundry Times: The Comparison of Religions (London: Faber & Faber, 1958),
p. 12.

[8]W. Kristensen, The Meaning of Religion, from
the Foreword by Heindrik Kraemer, xxiv.

"Science of Religion" operates under presuppositions. This makes the theological approach to man's religions legitimate and inevitable. If one cannot help entering the normative realm, then he should do so openly. When one's presuppositions are placed in clear view, then the theologian can be free of a false attitude of "scientific objectivity." Kraemer's goal is not to plead for complete objectivity, but to offer a more scientific approach which means making one's theological assumptions explicit from the start.

Nevertheless, the attitude of Kraemer should not indicate that there is a necessary conflict between a phenomenology and a theology of religions, and more specifically for our purposes, a Christian theology of religions. They actually should work hand in hand while leaving proper room for the proper object of each discipline. Those investigations which are conducted strictly as history and phenomenology of religion are of greatest importance for the theology of religions. In fact the description and comparison of religions is indispensable for the theology of religions. But the theology of religions is not and cannot be the general science of religion. This means that in its handling of the findings of the history of religions, the theology of religions is justified in constantly comparing the facts with the statements of Christian faith, and in interpreting them on a basis of Christian theological self-awareness. Such a confrontation of the facts of the history of religion with Christian revelation and theology would not, of course, be undertaken primarily with apologetic intentions, for it requires a high degree of self-critical and methodical objectivity.[9]

The specialist in the science of religion will inevitably point out that the introduction of theological principles infringes objectivity as this is understood by the secular science of religion. This is in fact the case, and as has been mentioned, is not only unavoidable, but is expressly intended when it is a question of constituting a theology of religions. This point should be emphasized, so that

---

[9]H. R. Schlette, Towards a Theology of Religions (New York: Herder & Herder, 1966), p. 55.

the theology of religions will not mistake its method and results for the phenomenology of religion, nor conversely cause the latter to contest the legitimacy of statements of the theology of religions.

These distinctions have been introduced because they are important in understanding how Professor Zaehner proceeds. He works on different levels at different times, sometimes as an exegete, sometimes as a theologian. We are trying to establish that it is legitimate for him to work on the theological, normative level of understanding. It is part of his scholarly prerogative to weigh, to compare, to judge, to ask whether such and such a view about ultimate reality is true and worthy of allegiance. In fact the endeavour is commendable since his conclusions are contributions to the understanding and possible unity of religions.

Faced with the fact of the diversity of the great religions, Zaehner's question is how does one approach this problem without doing violence to any of the religions involved? It is important to be as accurate and objective as possible, although in Zaehner's view neither quality is totally attainable. Zaehner says: "objectivity sounds all very fine in theory, and it is possible to write books on religion with what appears to be rigorous impartiality . . . complete objectivity is never attainable in practice except in minute points of scholarship."[10] His reason for saying this is that in interpreting a religion or a sacred book one is bound to interpret, whether one admits it or not. Why? Because previous interpretations, or one's own theological bias, or general frame of reference have to influence the interpreter.

Zaehner admits that this is the case even in the books which he has written on Zoroastrianism which might be considered his "objective" works. His point is that even in writing a descriptive, "objective" book one has to select what one considers to be most important, thus ending total objectivity.

---

[10]R. C. Zaehner, Concordant Discord: The Interdependence of Faiths, Being the Gifford Lectures 1967-69 (London: Oxford University Press, 1970), p. 9.

The problem of objectivity is even more pronounced in the case of a religion as complex as Hinduism. How does one treat the changes occurring in its history or the nuances of its thought in one volume? Zaehner's attempt to express the centrality of Hinduism led him to emphasize its movement from pantheism towards monotheism. Based on the evidence, as he sees it, this movement is the major trend in the historical development of Hinduism. Is this a correct evaluation? Or has Zaehner's theistic and Christian subjective mind led him to see the evidence that way? The objection is valid and Zaehner's response would be twofold: First, previous convictions can influence even the scholar's attitude. All that he can humanly do is guard against this influence and try to deceive himself as little as possible. Secondly, one should consider the difficulty that the sacred texts pose for the objective minded scholar: "Sacred books, however, rarely show any obvious consistency: they refuse to be pigeon-holed. Any system that claims to derive from them therefore, must distort them at some point. The function of the modern commentator who does aim at objectivity, then, should be to accept the inconsistencies as they stand, to see them in historical perspective, and to try to follow any trend of ideological development they may or may not display.[11] But to have some kind of commitment need not be detrimental. As Professor Benjamin Schwartz mentions:

> While these commitments are bound to color his [the scholar's] understanding to some extent, he can make an effort to distinguish in his own mind between his commitments and his attempts to understand the conscious response of others. On the other hand, the illusion of complete non-involvement, with all the self-deceptions it nourishes, is more detrimental to objectivity than a lively sense of involvement controlled by the desire to understand.[12]

---

[11] Ibid., p. 10.

[12] B. Schwartz, "The Intellectual History of China" in Chinese Thought and Institutions, ed. John Fairbank, quoted in J. M. Kitagawa, The History of Religions, p. 28.

Unity and Disunity Among World Religions

As far back as 1953, in his inaugural lecture as Spalding Professor of Eastern religions and ethics, Professor Zaehner commented on the apparent lack of unity and harmony between major world religions. "Nor do I think that it can be a legitimate function of a university professor to attempt to induce harmony among elements as disparate as the great religions of mankind appear to be, if, as seems inevitable, the resultant harmony is only to be apparent, verbal and therefore fictitious."[13] In the same lecture he also noted: "It is only too true that the basic principles of Eastern and Western, which in practice means Indian and Semitic, thought are not irreconcilably opposed; they are simply not starting from the same premises. . . . The great religions are talking at cross purposes."[14]

We will return to the contrast of East and West shortly.

Professor Zaehner has been adamant in a conviction of a lack of a fundamental unity underlying all the great religions. This was his position through the 1950s and he has maintained the position through the late 1960s in his Gifford Lectures of 1967-69. Too much of the "harmony" seen by some in comparative religion has only been, in Zaehner's words, "apparent, verbal and therefore fictitious. . . . We must force nothing we must not try to achieve a harmony of religions at all costs."[16] Concordant discord at this early stage of contact with the non-Christian religions is surely the most

---

[13]R. C. Zaehner, Foolishness to the Greeks: An Inaugural Lecture at Oxford University on November 2, 1953, Appendix in Zaehner, Concordant Discord, p. 429.

[14]Ibid., p. 439.

[15]R. C. Zaehner, Christianity and Other Religions (New York: Hawthorn & Co., 1964), p. 15.

[16]Zaehner, Concordant Discord, p. 7.

we can hope for.

Zaehner asks a question in imaginative terms:
what constitutes the concordant discord which the
orchestra of religions is trying to bring to our
ears? Of what is it composed? In answering, his
subjective penchant is evident in a willingness to
choose one element for which he has sympathy. By-
passing philosophy, poetry, devotional literature,
artistic, historical, social and structural expression in religion, he chooses texts that each religion
holds most sacred and the impact these have caused.
In these texts one finds harmonies far more profound
and discords far more telling than one is likely to
meet with in philosophic systems.[17] This is
evidence of Zaehner's being the exegete, the linguist, before being the theologian.

In principle, Zaehner feels that it is right
to stress the discord rather than the concord of
religions. It is the duty of the scholar first to
analyse the differences, and only then to look for
a possible synthesis which might make some sense of
the heterogeneous elements analysed. Yet this stress
on discord is not to be viewed negatively. It is
not differences that are ultimately important but
mutual enrichment. "Thus in our approach to the
non-Christian religions we waste our time in pin-
pointing the differences that separate us since
they are obvious enough: rather we must seek to
understand them from within and try to grasp how
they too seek to penetrate the mystery of our being
and our eternal destiny; for they too have a magnif-
icent heritage of ripe spirituality from which
Christians can learn and profit."[18]

This latter element is introduced to show
that Zaehner sees the concord as well as discord
between religions. Religious unity may be a thing
of the far distant future. But he sees the value
of stressing present harmony and mutual enrichment.

This element of mutual enrichment and respect is present even when Zaehner speaks from the

---

[17]Ibid., p. 19.

[18]Zaehner, Christianity and Other Religions,
p. 8.

14

viewpoint of Roman Catholicism. He asserts what is now taken for granted viz. that non-Christian religions contain truth in one or more of its manifold aspects. The early church had always understood that all truth, wherever we find it, must proceed from God.

Echoing the teaching of Vatican II Zaehner rejects nothing that is true or holy in any religion. One can only have respect in the face of Truth.[19]

"The Catholic Church has been slow indeed to welcome and acclaim all the truth that any man of good will can descry in the Eastern Religions."[20] Zaehner's terminology is indicative of a true attitude of ecumenism. The truth can be found in eastern religions. It is not a question then of the truth being found in the one true religion viz. Catholicism. So, he does not pit true religion against a false religion in an either-or dilemma. Thus Zaehner writes: "It seems to be that the Indian religions in particular have something to teach us and that this something can help us deepen our own religion and open up insights that were only dimly perceived before."[21]

Zaehner is convinced that there is much in Eastern religions that is still valid, and that Christianity has much to learn from them, much indeed it must learn from them if it is ever to become, not in name only but in truth, the Catholic Church designated by its founder to become the religion of the whole human race. "Catholics . . . have come to see how greatly the Eastern techniques of meditation . . . can expand and deepen their own Christian life of prayer."[22]

---

[19]Zaehner, Concordant Discord, p. 13.

[20]Zaehner, Christianity and Other Religions, p. 130.

[21]Zaehner, Concordant Discord, p. 19.

[22]Zaehner, Christianity and Other Religions, p. 130.

Gandhi was a man of God, and he was also a man who saw good in all religions. He was not ashamed to learn from Christianity and Islam, nor was he blind to the sometimes hideous defects of his own religion. He learnt much from Christianity, and with his example before us we should be presumptuous fools to think that we, as Catholics, have nothing to learn from him and from the whole religious tradition that made him possible.[23]

Nevertheless, even the Council statements of Vatican II have limited value for Zaehner. They do not point the way to an eventual harmony of religions even though they contain a suggestion of the possibility of this harmony. The problem is that the differences between religions have been glossed over. In Zaehner's eyes the eirenic spirit of the Council emphasizes religious harmony, and some harmony there is. But one must be frank enough to acknowledge the basic discord in this concord, "a discord between what each religion has come to believe to be the very core of its teaching."[24]

In Zaehner's method there is also further room for contrasting religions. He divides the major world religions into two groups. This is done, first of all, to emphasize the differences or discord between the religions. But Zaehner also wants to show that there are religions that fall midway between these two types of religion, blending elements from both sides. He opines that Christianity is one of these midway religions. He will argue later that Christianity of all the religions best fulfills the religious aspirations of these two major groups.

What are these two groups? They are: 1) the Hebraic and Islamic prophetic religions and 2) the mystical religions or traditions. Admittedly the division is arbitrary enough and done for the sake of clarification; an attempt to correlate religions in a more or less orderly pattern. He says: "I do not pretend that this is necessarily the right way to deal with the problem. For me it is the only way,

---

[23]Ibid., p. 57.

[24]Zaehner, Concordant Discord, p. 15.

16

for this is the way I have come to see things."[25]

For all three Semitic religions God is a transcendent reality who is vitally concerned with the doings of men in this world. He commands and prohibits demanding obedience; he makes known his will through the prophets whom he himself chooses. The prophet brings a message from a highly personal God whom he is unable to control. The prophet is convinced of his experience of a direct contact with God. The message is one of threat or consolation, sin, God's will, salvation.

Judaism (and its daughter faiths) is distinguished by the fact that its sacred book is, in theory at least, a history book: it is a progressive revelation made by a highly personal God in time, and the revelation comes through a whole series of prophets in the cause of history. Other religions are based on a structure of myth which tends to a greater independence of time. "It is a symbol of something that is thought to be eternal: it is something ever renewed or re-enacted in ritual . . . bringing man into direct contact with the eternal processes of renewal both in the cosmos and in himself. And it was this that the Hebrew prophets were reacting against."[26]

The God of the Jews was not merely the God of Nature. He was the one true God who reveals Himself to His chosen people. He is a jealous God and this exclusivity has characterized Judaism and also Christianity and Islam Her daughter faiths.

In the Semitic tradition man is born once and for all into a life with beginning, middle, end: he lives one life only and is rewarded or punished for what he does in that one life. In Indian religion time is cyclic, i.e., it moves in ever recurring cycles from eternity without beginning to eternity without end. There is no final rest, for the cosmic process has no end. Unless he is shown a way of escape man remains in this process. Life itself then becomes an evil from which escape must be sought. Transmigration is so deeply rooted in India that it is not proved but assumed as a self-evident fact. Thus Indian religion is not so

[25]Ibid., p. 19.   [26]Ibid., p. 24.

17

concerned with the existence of God or obedience to
His will as it is with practical ways of escaping
from the eternal round of ever-recurring birth and
death, re-birth and re-death.

For the Hindu, obedience to the will of God
is not the essential prerequisite of religion; indeed it can be said that for some Hindus it has
little relevance for him whether there is one God or
many or even if there is none at all. Salvation,
for him, does not mean primarily salvation from sin,
but salvation or rather liberation from our human
condition as such. Buddhism too, which is more
coherent than Hinduism, is even more emphatic on
this point, especially Theravada Buddhism.[27]

In mystical religions God appears especially
as immanent. Emphasis is on the possibility of discovery within oneself. The spiritual life is often
conceived of as an experience of cosmic communion.
This is in sharp contrast to the Semitic conception
of the transcendent God who reveals Himself, who
founds the spiritual life on an experience of communion with Himself.

A final contrast between the two types of
religion is based on varying views on salvation.

In an earlier work I contrasted prophetic religion with mystical religion, and I think the
contrast holds. You have only to compare the
immense emphasis Christian (and particularly
Protestant) theologians put on the "historicity"
of God--and contrast this with the overriding
insistence of the Vedantins on Brahman as pure
Being, and therefore unaffected by and indif-
ferent to what goes on in this world, to realize
that between these two points of view there is
a gulf fixed. But this is not the only distinction we can draw between the higher religions:
there is another, and it is at least as important. On the one side there are religions
which concentrate mainly on individual salvation
or "liberation," and on the other there are
those which see salvation as being applicable

---

[27]Zaehner, Christianity and Other Religions,
p. 16.

mainly to the group, nation, Empire, or ultimately the whole human race. Both Hinduism and
Buddhism seem to be overwhelmingly individual-
istic so far as "salvation" is concerned, whereas Confucianism, Judaism, and Islam think
primarily in terms of the community.[28]

Thus, Zaehner divides the major world religions into two major groups. There is only one common point in the religions, exclusive of the ethical
sphere: the existence of the eternal and a preoccupation with eternity. The eternal can be understood
as an eternal being outside man--God, or else as
the eternity of man's own being--immortality. Other
than that he sees wide divergences between the two
groups, at times to the point of antithesis.[29]

Zaehner distinguishes these groups to show
their differences. But he also does so to show that
certain religions take a middle position between
the two poles. Prophetic religion teaches how God
wills that we should act in this world. Mystical
religion, on the other hand, brings us experience
of another world that transcends this one, for it
transcends space and time by which this world is
conditioned. More generally, the two types of religion could be described as this-worldly and other-
worldly religions. Judaism, Islam, Protestantism,
and Confucianism are predominantly this-worldly
religions, stressing as they do the need for righteous conduct here on earth; Hinduism, Theravada
Buddhism, and Taoism are predominantly other-worldly
religions, insisting all the time that there is a
timeless reality or experience beyond this world
which it is in man's power to reach. In between the
extremes stand Mahayana Buddhism, Neo-Confucianism,
the reformed Hinduism of Gandhi and Tagore, and the
Catholic Church. "I have purposely not discussed
the standing of Christianity in the overall picture
of the prophetic Semitic tradition because

---

[28]R. C. Zaehner, Evolution in Religion: A
Study in Sri Aurobindo and Teilhard de Chardin (London: Oxford University Press, 1971), p. 91.

[29]R. C. Zaehner, The Concise Encyclopedia of
Living Faiths (Boston: Beacon Press, 1959), p. 204.

Christianity is not by any means exclusively a prophetic religion. For both the Jews and the Muslims,
the figure of Christ as depicted in the New Testament must be a scandal since for both the idea of an
incarnate "Son of God" is blasphemous."[30]

For Christians then Jesus is God made man,
and this makes it impossible to treat Christianity
simply as a prophetic religion. From the very beginning a mystical element is present, and it is this
if anything that entitles Christianity to speak of
itself as unique. It cannot be broadly classified
as either prophetic or mystical: it combines the
two.

The Question of a "Higher Synthesis" of Religions

While considering questions of similarity
and dissimilarity between major world religions
Zaehner legitimately raises the question of the possibility of a "higher synthesis" of world religions.[31]
The question is raised for two reasons: First of all
there are teachers such as Jung, Ramakrishna, Radhakrishnan, who claim that all religions are true.
For Zaehner this is equivalent to saying that none
of them are true. In particular Zaehner rejects the
religious unity resulting from the theory of his
predecessor at Oxford, Sir Sarvepalli Radhakrishnan.
This theory was a form of Vedantin monism--reality
is one and all multiplicity is therefore to some
extent illusory, being no more than an appearance.
Thus, according to Zaehner Vedantin monism considers
itself as the ultimate Truth, and all religions are
simply empirical paths leading towards this same
Truth.

In Zaehner's eyes though, such a position
leaves wholly out of account the core and center of
the non-Indian religions. Even further Zaehner
opines that Radhakrishnan's view of religious harmony
could only be sustained by misquotation of non-Indian

---

[30]Zaehner, Concordant Discord, pp. 29-30.

[31]Zaehner, Concise Encyclopedia of Living
Faiths, p. 414.

scriptures. Such a harmony is valueless to Zaehner because it is based on a fundamental misunderstanding.[32]

And at the same time it should not be overlooked that such a view (of Hinduism) is not so universal as appears on the surface. It does not ultimately allow for a harmony between world religions. It asks one to accept one particular sect of one religion, viz. Vedantin monism.

Zaehner would agree with the remark of Hans Kung concerning the identity of all religions.

> But when he simplifies this identity to the point of asserting that all articulate religious statements, all revelations and confessions of faith, all authorities and rites are relative, and the only thing that has any ultimate validity is that inner spiritual experience of the absolute which appears in different forms in all religions, and can never be adequately expressed, then he is taking up a dogmatic standpoint. It is only possible to make all religions equal if the underlying formless, mystical experience is being set up as an absolute.[33]

The second reason for raising the question of a religious synthesis is because men like Arnold Toynbee and G. E. Moore view religions as expressions of essential truths. These common truths can be distilled from major religions leading to a common denominator of world religions. In effect a new religion is created which is the sum total of the basic truths which all major world religions propose. Religions are expressions of essential truths; their differences are concerned merely with non-essentials. Thus Toynbee lists in broad generalizations seven truths common to the major world religions.[34] These

---

[32]Zaehner, Concordant Discord, p. 7.

[33]Hans Kung as quoted by Baird, Category Formation and the History of Religions, p. 121.

[34]Arnold Toynbee, An Historian's Approach to Religion (New York: Scribner, 1956), pp. 273ff. The common truths are 1) Man himself is certainly not

21

become the basis for unity and harmony among the
religions.

This view of a "higher synthesis" of religions is attractive and on the face of it problem-
solving. Men of all faiths could supposedly be
joined by the essentials of all religions. The
points of disagreement would be of only secondary
importance, matter for the professional theologians.

But Zaehner rejects a "higher synthesis" as
a solution to the dialogue of world religions. Why?
His basic reason is that what Toynbee regards as
essential "truths" of religion are not common even
to the seven religions with which he deals. The
"truths" are rejected in part by some religions, or
are not accepted by other religions, are not true
when applied to certain religions, or can only be
accepted with great nuancing. The problem is that
one tries to fit all religions into categories
which ultimately do not apply. The subtlety and
complexity of religions are too great for neat
categorizing. Further, one does not do justice to
any one religion by imposing on it arbitrary
standards from without. "Professor Toynbee's essential truths unfortunately do not coincide with the
facts: he is making the great religions say what
he personally thinks they ought to say."[35]

Nor does Zaehner think that the differences

---

the greatest spiritual presence in the universe. 2)
There is a presence in the universe that is spiritually greater than man himself. 3) In human life,
knowledge is not an end in itself, but is a means to
action. 4) Man's goal is to seek communion with the
presence behind the phenomena, and to seek it with
the aim of bringing himself into harmony with the
absolute spiritual reality. 5) A human self cannot
be brought into harmony with absolute reality unless
it can get rid of its innate self-centredness. This
is the hardest task that man can set himself. 6)
Absolute reality has both an impersonal and a personal aspect. 7) The personal aspect of 'God' must
be good as well as omnipotent.

[35]Zaehner, Concise Encyclopedia of Living
Faiths, p. 414.

between religions are concerned merely with non-essentials. As mentioned earlier, the differences are real indicating significantly different religious attitudes. One can gloss over the differences lightly. But this is not to do full justice to any one particular religion. The significant difference of one religion from another can constitute the genius of a particular religion. The fact is that differences can point to essential disunity. However much Toynbee may bewail what he calls the "group selfishness" of the great religions, this "group selfishness" is inherent in any religion which believes itself to be true, and is, in fact, what gives it life. Certainly each of the prophetic religions believes itself to be uniquely true. It is however equally true that the Buddha claimed that "there is one sole way for the purification of beings" and that "truth is one, there is not a second." Buddhism, then as originally propounded, is as exclusive as are the three great monotheistic religions of Semitic origin.[36]

Furthermore, in Zaehner's opinion Professor Toynbee's equation of Christianity with Mahayana Buddhism completely misses the point. Buddhism in all its forms is a religion of escape--of escape from the world of samsara where all is pain and suffering. Christianity is a religion which sanctifies matter and elevates it to the realm of spirit. "At the same time it bids us accept this world with all its transient joys and sorrows, to grasp the nettle of this world of pain, to take up our cross, not to try to discover how we can rid ourselves of it."[37]

It is then, methodologically quite wrong to treat the great religions of the world as parallel phenomena, and to saddle all of them, as Professor Toynbee does, with purely subjective "essential truths." It is also unhistorical, since it makes no attempt to distinguish between the essentials of any given religion.

One thing, however, seems certain: the differences that separate the great religions will not,

---

[36]Ibid., p. 414.   [37]Ibid., p. 417.

in the foreseeable future, suddenly evaporate into
any "higher synthesis," but will continue to preach
their different messages, seeking to save and com-
fort souls according to what they believe. Echoing
the words of Hendrik Kraemer, Zaehner remarks that
"what is needed in the present time of world-
encounter of religions, is not to be as sweet as
possible with each other, but to learn the art of
being as true as possible with each other, in spiritual emulation."[38]

Christ as the Coherent Pattern
of Religious History

Thus far we have discussed Zaehner's basic
attitudes towards inter-religious dialogue. This
has uncovered some of his convictions as well as his
reservations about theories that in his opinion lead
only to a false harmony. So the question remains:
what is Zaehner's viewpoint on the possibility of
religious unity? Does he have a positive opinion
to offer to the world community of religious believers? He states his conviction quite clearly:
"In all my writings on comparative religion my aim
has been increasingly to show that there is a
coherent pattern in religious history. For me the
center of coherence can only be Christ."[39]

The Incarnation of Christ then, is central
in the inter-religious dialogue. So it has been
since the time he assumed his post at Oxford. In
his inaugural lecture he wrote:

And this seems to me to constitute one fundamental difference between Christianity and the
Eastern non-Christian religions. Christianity

---

[38]Ibid. But note that Zaehner is not to be
associated with the theological stance of Kraemer.
In a conversation with Zaehner at All Souls College,
Oxford, on May 30th, 1972 he mentioned that Kraemer
was a fine scholar but that his view of world religions was too one-sided in favor of Christianity and
too narrowly based on Christian scripture.

[39]Zaehner, Concordant Discord, p. 16.

bases itself firmly on the doctrine of Incarnation, the doctrine that God became man to deliver mankind from sin and to reconcile him with Himself. There is nothing comparable to this in the sacred books of the Hindus, the Buddhists, or the Moslems--or, for that matter, of the Confucians and Taoists. Yet the later developments of the first three of these religions show that each has evolved, independently it would appear, a theory of divine incarnation and of a divine mediator between God and man.[40]

Zaehner works on the theme of the Incarnate God who came to make all things one in himself, "reconciling the world unto himself."

Zaehner anticipates the objection that one does not need this reconciliation. Why is there no need? Simply because the mystics of all times and all religions, or of no religion, testify to the oneness of all things and of eternal harmony which, once we see it as we should, is here and now among us. Zaehner admits that this harmony is there and pervades all created things. He attributes it to their being grounded in the Holy Spirit. But even so, does it matter to have visions and sensations of a universal harmony and a universal peace? The insight of the nature mystic, of the Taoist, or of the Confucian does not produce a peace or harmony in this world of space and time. It is, rather, a vision of the harmony of the universe experienced perhaps once in a lifetime, by one in a hundred human beings. The insight is valuable but unfortunately the discord, misery and strife in which we live are no less real. In effect, then, Zaehner is saying that the real world of pain and living needs something or someone as a reconciler.[41]

What type of reconciliation does Zaehner envisage? Christ's mission was to bring together all things that had been separated by sin. First he must make the human being whole himself, for only

---

[40] Zaehner, _Foolishness to the Greeks_, p. 442.

[41] Zaehner, _Christianity and Other Religions_, pp. 134-35.

then can he offer him back to the Father in the same perfection in which he was made. Christ, the second Adam, is crucified that the first Adam, living on in his children as their "transcendent self" may be crucified with him, due to pride, and resurrect in perfect charity. The inner Eve, too--the "empirical" soul--must be reintegrated into her redeemed consort, the transcendent self, and through him into Christ and God.

Who needs reconciliation? Man, whose relationship with his God, with himself, with his fellow men, and his universe, has been ruptured. For Zaehner this is the meaning of the Fall and Original Sin. In his fallen state man is estranged from the transcendent, incapable of recovering from this estrangement on his own. Without divine intervention and divine revelation man can go no further than realize the timeless wonder of his own soul. And God has made this revelation in both East and West. Both the Gita for the Hindu and the Lotus Sutra for the Buddhist agree in this, that the realization of one's own soul is but the beginning of the way; both agree that it is love that brings the soul into the presence of the unknown God. Asia had thus been well prepared for the hearing of the good news that God had actually become man in history in the person of Jesus Christ.[42]

Thus it is evident that Zaehner views Christ as the fulfillment of religious man's deepest aspirations. Christ came not to destroy but to fulfill all the insights into the nature of divine truth that God had scattered throughout the world. For Zaehner it is the meaning of the exclamation: "O testimonium animae naturaliter Christianae." "It seems to be indeed true that all man's highest aspirations in the farther East, as in Jewry, point with increasing urgency to the Incarnation of the Righteous and Loving God."[43] Christ is not only the true Messiah, but also the true Krishna, and the true Bodhisattva who takes upon himself the burden of saving all sentient beings until the end of time.

Zaehner also sees Jesus as the teacher of a perfectly balanced religion. Seen objectively, says Zaehner, Jesus is the founder of one of the

---

[42]Ibid., p. 143.   [43]Ibid., p. 146.

26

three world religions which have withstood the test
of time--the other two being, Gautama the Buddha and
Muhammad. Ideologically he stands midway between
the other two: Christ is the middle point between
the kingdom of God within us, the Nirvana of the
Buddhists, and the city of God on earth, the theo-
cracy of the four orthodox Caliphs which all Sunni
Muslims look back to as the only true Muslim
society.[44]

Buddhism too considers itself to be the Middle Way, the middle way between excessive asceticism
and self-indulgence; but Christ too is the "middle"
Way, Truth, and Light between the ways, truths, and
lights of Buddhism and Islam, just as the Gita is
the middle way between the absolute monism of the
non-dualist Vedanta and the absolute dualism of the
Samkhya. The Gita is middle ground since it sees
salvation in terms of matter as well as spirit.
For Zaehner this insight of the Gita takes place in
a pre-eminent way in the Incarnation of Christ.
This Incarnation is a new creation; the appearance
of the all-man, destined to be the focus of all
human matter that can be spiritualized and saved.

Finally, Zaehner stresses the pre-eminence
of the person, Christ. Christianity is not just a
message. As beautiful as it is, for example, one
cannot point to the Sermon on the Mount as the expression of Christianity. It is quite as Buddhist
as it is Christian. Rather, "the preacher," it was
claimed, was also God, the Word, the second person
of the Holy Trinity, the Cit of the Sanskrit Trinitarian formula: sac-cid ananda, the principle of
rationality and order through and in which the universe coheres and follows eternal and unchanging
laws. Hence it was the second Person of the Holy
Trinity, the Logos, who had to become incarnate
since man, as Aurobindo says in a telling phrase,
"is an abnormal who has not found his own normality," i.e., his own Logos. The Logos made man,
therefore, is the purely human normality of man
presented to him both as a doctrine and, much more
essentially, as a human life, lived in flagrant
opposition to all the received standards of the

---

[44]Zaehner, Evolution in Religion, p. 69.

"world," standards dictated by egoism.[45]

Here we have a life which is the absolute
antithesis of the kind of life the Jews expected
from their Messiah, a life of humility, self-efface-
ment, of absolute and deliberate rejection of all the
accepted social norms and of superficiality in all
its manifold disguises, of hardship, and finally
in Gethsemane of spiritual anguish and near-despair.
This is why Zaehner starts with, not the cosmic
Christ of St. Paul as developed by Teilhard de
Chardin, but the man, Jesus of Nazareth, son of Mary.
"Thus God becomes man in order that man may become
God. But you cannot become God until you become
like the man who God became--Jesus, son of Mary."[46]

Briefly then, Zaehner views the Christian
Incarnation as central to his theology. Jesus is
the one who in becoming man reconciles all things
and all people to himself. It is Christ who ultimately fulfills man's deepest religious aspirations.
He does this by teaching a balanced, mid-path in religious belief. It is he who is pre-eminent, the model
of what God wants all of us to be.

Whether or not these claims can be substan-
tiated will be examined more critically in chapter
two.

The Church as a Possible Center
of Religious Unity

Zaehner's writings assign a definite role to
the Catholic Church in the dialogue with other major
world religions. This will be treated in detail in
chapter three. His view of the Church is mentioned
here to indicate Zaehner's methodology. Our purpose
then is to understand why Zaehner introduces an
ecclesial element into his system of thought and
what this adds to his view of religious unity.

For Zaehner Christ is the central point of
religious history. It is only when he has established
his Christology in the context of world religions that
he introduces the role of the Church. "Christ, the

---

[45]Ibid., p. 74.   [46]Ibid., p. 75.

28

new Adam, then, was the focus around which a new, regenerated humanity was to take shape: he is the 'head' of his own body, which was to be the Church."[47]

The Church then is to be the Church of the Word incarnate, the Word Who continues to reconcile the world unto Himself. This is the collective Christ, or as Zaehner mentions frequently, the Communion of Saints. ". . . the ideal of a society as tightly knit together as in a human body, the body of the man-God Christ himself, dead and resurrected in the Church he had founded. This was the substance of the Catholic Church and of the Catholic idea--the idea of coherence and totality in one living organism that one day was to embrace the whole world."[48]

The Church also serves as a center of unity in the frame of which the collective salvation of mankind can one day be realized. Although Zaehner admits the foibles of the Church, still in its structure and gospel, it contains a message of universal appeal. It is a possible center of unity for mankind; whether this goal is ever achieved depends on the Church's ability to realize Christ's message of faith, hope and love. And this latter point again shows Zaehner's view of the Church in relation to Christ. "The Christian Church even now represents only a fraction of mankind, but ideally the body of Christ should encompass the whole human race--how and in what form-- we have not the slightest idea."[49]

The point that should be emphasized however is that the Church's destiny is to rebuild mankind into the image and unity of Christ. It is not to work for the conquest of one religion over another. Christ is central. Should the Church be a source of unity, so be it. But should it become more of an obstacle than a hindrance, then ecclesial presence must cede to Christ. This is not to say that Christ and Church are opposites. As stated, the Church, the communion of saints, is at least the theoretical locus of the continuing Incarnation of

---

[47]Ibid., p. 106.   [48]Ibid., pp. 87-88.

[49]Ibid., p. 112.

Christ. The conclusion will indicate that at the present time the weight of dialogue on the Christian side should rest on Christ and not the Church.

Zaehner also sees the Church, as well as Christ, as the fulfillment of man's spiritual aspirations. This he will investigate in man's search for a balance between divine transcendence and immanence in relation to man. The same method is followed in his study of man's search for individual salvation vis-à-vis communal salvation or solidarity. The Church strikes a balance between these aspirations and thus fulfills these religious desires of mankind. The model is again fulfillment. This too will be discussed critically in chapters three and five.

A final point on Church and methodology concerns the role of other religions in regard to Christianity. Zaehner sees Catholic Christianity in terms of evolution leading to a unity and convergence among major world religions. But he notes that each of the religions has or will have its distinctive and individual part to play. This attitude separates him from a "triumphalist" or "conversion oriented" mentality. All the world religions are to be taken seriously because of their own genuineness and because of mutual enrichment. Hence, Zaehner may propose a fulfillment theme for Christianity but does not suggest the demise of the uniqueness of other religious groups.

In this context it will be well to mention a point to be treated more at length later, viz. Zaehner's attitude toward revelation in all religions. We are not that far past a time when non-Christian religions were viewed as "pagan" or "erroneous." For Zaehner, though, revelation is not limited to Christianity. God has revealed Himself before the time of Christianity and outside of Christianity. Thus he writes: "Without divine intervention and divine revelation man can go no further than to realize the timeless wonder of his soul, but such a divine revelation was granted to the Hindus in the Gita."[50]

---

[50]Zaehner, Christianity and Other Religions, pp. 140-41.

30

Briefly, then, Zaehner's attitude towards the
Catholic Church and other religions is the following.
First, Jesus Christ is the central point of dialogue.
The Church as a continuation of his incarnation is a
possible center of unity but subordinate to Christ.
Its structures of universality and solidarity are
important elements to consider in world unity.
Secondly, the church is seen as a possible fulfillment of the spiritual aspirations of mankind. This
is not to overlook its deficiencies. Thirdly, all
of the world religions have their importance. Each
one adds to religious dialogue and unity. They are
true vehicles of God's revelation to mankind.

Thus far we have seen that Zaehner's basic
methodology is that of the theologian of religions,
or as he says, the comparative study of religions.
He feels that it is necessary to probe and compare
religions in order to arrive at a better appreciation of their various claims. Although the religions
evidence great diversity, and although Zaehner rejects an unacceptable synthesis of religions, this
does not preclude a unifying theme among the religions. The unifying element, the coherent pattern
among world religions is found, in Zaehner's view,
in Jesus Christ and the community that bears his
name. This is how Zaehner has come to view things
after years of study, even if it is an admittedly
Christian viewpoint. It is his theological understanding of the unifying thread among the religions.
Since the role of Jesus Christ is the most important
part of Zaehner's insight, it constitutes the basis
for our next chapter.

CHAPTER II

THE CENTRALITY OF CHRIST IN ZAEHNER'S THOUGHT

The Uniqueness of Christ and His Incarnation in Religious History

There is no doubt that in Zaehner's mind the Incarnation of Christ is central in inter-religious dialogue. Christ is the coherent pattern of religious history. He is, says Zaehner, unique in all of religious history, unique in his person, his life and his message. Owing to this uniqueness Christ is the fulfillment of the religious aspirations of man.

The uniqueness of Christian Incarnation lies in the fact that it is the basis of Christianity and essential to its orthodox teaching. The Hindu, Buddhist and Islamic religions do not insist on a divine incarnate figure, a mediator and reconciler, as part of their essential or even orthodox teaching. It is true that each of these religions has evolved a theory of divine incarnation and mediatorship. But in all of these religions except Christianity, the theory develops in logical opposition to the dominant view of each of the sacred books. So, if the major religions have a theory of incarnation it is a similarity between Christian orthodoxy and non-Christian heterodoxy. The similarity proves, not that there is an inner unity underlying all the great world religions, but that there is in man a craving for an incarnate God strong enough to force its way into a religious system where it seemed to have no rightful place.

So Zaehner feels that the different origins and positions of incarnation within religious systems are significant. Indeed, the idea of incarnation seems important to the believers of all these religions. Then Christianity has an especially strong point inasmuch as the incarnation is the cornerstone of its belief. Incarnation is essentially at variance with all the non-Christian

orthodoxies. "Its [the Incarnation's] constant re-
appearance demonstrates the truth of Tertullian's
saying: 'O Testimonium Animae Naturaliter Christianae.' The difference is that whereas Muhammad
and the Buddha achieved deification in flat contra-
diction to what they claimed and wished, and whereas
the incarnations of Vishnu have no basis in fact,
Jesus Christ both lived and died, and claimed to be
the Son of God."[1]

Zaehner's next point is to show that Christ
is the model of the religious life that all men are
to lead. Christ's coming has had a purpose. It
has shown us the type of life God wants all men to
lead. Thus "God became man that we might partake
of his divinity in order that man may become God.
But he cannot become God until he becomes like the
man who God became--Jesus, son of Mary."[2]

Jesus the historical son of Mary, was to be
the second all-man, destined to be the focus of all
human matter that can be spiritualized and saved,
the Superman of both Aurobindo and de Chardin. He
is God, the Word, the second person of the Trinity,
the cit of the Sanskrit Trinitarian formula sac-cit
ananda, the principle of rationality and order
through and in which the universe coheres and follows
eternal and unchanging laws. He becomes the Logos
for man who has not found his own normality, i.e.,
his own Logos. The Logos made man, is the purely
human normality of man presented to him both as a
doctrine and, much more essentially, as a human
life, lived in opposition to all the received standards dictated by all the egoism of the Fall.[3]

The notion of God becoming incarnate on earth
would be, in Zaehner's view, psychologically true;
for the true nature of God can only be made compre-
hensible to man if it is presented in human form.
All the major religions that are not atheistical
hold that God in His essence is ultimately incompre-
hensible to the intellect. Nor could He or can He
be even partially comprehended unless He manifests

---

[1]Zaehner, Concordant Discord, p. 443.

[2]Zaehner, Evolution in Religion, p. 75.

[3]Ibid., p. 74.

Himself in human form. And if He does this, then
this Man-God must be what Jung calls psychologically
true.[4]

In Jesus, God became man not to save man
from the world but to sanctify man in the world: to
sanctify man's frustration and suffering and failure
by the example of his own frustration and suffering
and failure. But God did not just become man, the
Eternal did not enter the temporal so that man
should drop out of the temporal: he became Jesus
of Nazareth, the sort of man who, in his humility
and compassion, his spontaneity and hatred of all
self-righteousness, in his acceptance of suffering
and his experience of dereliction and despair, showed
us the sort of man God wants us to be.[5]

Zaehner also argues that to accept the example of Christ is to accept His unique nature. If,
for instance, you accept the Christian ethic as being
the noblest, are you justified in rejecting Christ's
claim to be the Son of God, since it is that very
claim that gives to Christian ethics whatever validity they may possess? For if Christ is, as Christians claim, the Only Begotten Son of God, then
obviously his words must be unique and of unique
value. If, on the other hand, He is only one amongst
many manifestations of the deity, his claim to be the
Son of God must be false. To accept his teaching
without accepting his claims would therefore seem
illogical.[6]

This section has stated briefly Zaehner's

---

[4]R. C. Zaehner, Mysticism Sacred and Profane
(New York: Oxford University Press, Galaxy Reprint,
1957), p. 194.

[5]R. C. Zaehner, Drugs, Mysticism, and Make-
Believe (London: Collins Publishers, 1972), p. 210.

[6]R. C. Zaehner, "Dogma," The Hibbert Journal
53 (October 1954):16. Zaehner says elsewhere: "In
Christ, Christianity claims, God manifested Himself
perfectly . . . the moral stature of Christ is in-
finitely superior to that of the deities of the Hindu
pantheon." Mysticism Sacred and Profane, p. 207.

basic arguments on the importance of Christ's incarnation in relation to religious history. His emphasis on its uniqueness is evident. It could not be otherwise for him since Christ's claim to be true-God and true-man, sent by God, is central to Christianity. If it is a true claim then it is crucial for religious history. Chapter five will examine this claim critically. The question of uniqueness for religious thought needs also to be explored and applied to Christ's incarnation. It will also be necessary to see whether or not Zaehner's arguments are convincing to those who are not Christian believers.

Christ as the Fulfillment of Man's Religious Aspirations

A major part of Zaehner's method is to show Christ as the fulfillment of man's religious aspirations because of what He is and what He does. 1) Zaehner sees Christ as the fulfillment of the message of the prophets as well as the mystical insights of the east. 2) Christ is the center of all men's minds in their striving for solidarity. 3) Christ's message of universal love is foreshadowed at times in other religions. But this unique love brings to fulfillment certain deep religious motivations. Without it religious man is incomplete.

1) Zaehner has attempted to show how the main trend in Hinduism and Buddhism on the one hand (mystical religion) and of Zoroastrianism on the other (prophetic religion) meet and complete each other in the Christian revelation.

This view flows from Zaehner's conviction that Christ was truly the Son of God who brought God's word to man. From this point of view, i.e., Christ is the definitive moment in the religious history of man. Zaehner argues that other religions foreshadow Christ and find their fulfillment in him. The "immanentist" religions of India (and of Taoism in China too) do not contradict any essential Christian doctrine. Their representations of an incarnate God, incomplete though they are, are valid prefigurations of the God incarnate in Christ.[7]

---

[7]R. C. Zaehner, At Sundry Times: The

These prefigurations come to fruition since "Christ came not to destroy but to fulfill all the insights into the nature of divine truth that God had scattered throughout the world to guide men in their return to him out of this valley of tears."[8]

In an article which typifies his approach Zaehner examines some of the main insights of Hinduism, Buddhism and Zoroastrianism. These insights, in Zaehner's opinion, are confirmed and completed in Christ's Incarnation, especially in His death and resurrection. It will be sufficient to quote Zaehner's conclusion for it illustrates his method and shows the results of his comparative work:

> Thus it would seem that all the highest insights of the more ancient religions meet in Christianity. By dying for his friends Christ demonstrates the total quality of God's love for man as foreshadowed in the Bhagavad Gita and the Bodhisattva doctrine of Mahayana Buddhism; by ascending to the Father he shows that the destiny of the human soul, now that the rift between God and man has been healed, is no longer to be sought in isolation but in loving communion with God; and by the whole drama of the Incarnation and Resurrection he confirms the prophecy of Zoroaster, that, in the last days, man will be resurrected in body as well as in soul, and that he will live, as it was God's intention that he should, a harmonious whole within the greater whole of the totality of God's universe, communing for ever with his Maker, God.[9]

Christianity then does fulfill both the mystical tradition of India as finally expressed in the Bhagavad-Gita and the Bodhisattva doctrine, and the hopes of Zoroaster, the prophet of ancient Iran. In

---

Comparison of Religions (U. S. ed.; Boston: Beacon Press, 1962), p.11.

[8]Zaehner, Christianity and Other Religions, p. 146.

[9]R. C. Zaehner, "Christianity and the World Religions," Blackfriars 41 (August 1960):271.

Christ the two streams meet and are harmonized and reconciled as they are nowhere else for Christ fulfills both the law and the prophets in Israel and the gospel according to the Gentiles as it was preached in India and Iran.[10]

2) Christ also holds a pre-eminent place in religious history because He is the center of all men's minds and the central point of man's quest for solidarity. Thus Christ responds to two needs for unity: one in the individual himself and the other in terms of communal solidarity. Zaehner's view here is quite visionary instead of probative. Once again the vision flows from an acceptance of Christ's incarnation and its influence on mankind.

The Virgin Mary, says Zaehner, is the matter from which the new man is born. The Spirit had previously entered matter but this creation ultimately led to the Fall, to man's tendency to go it alone thwarting the tendency to unity. This tendency was an evaluation aimed at producing an association in which "the free development of each will be the condition for the free development of all." Such an association requires a center to hold it together and around which it can cohere. Hence in Zaehner's view the Holy Spirit's second descent into matter had to be into a single point or center--Christ.[11]

Christ died and rose from the dead, the man God, the Lord. But the resurrected and ascended Jesus is not just the Lord in heaven, he is also the indwelling God, the life that lives in us, the "Person" who is exhalted beyond Atman-Brahman, the true center of every creature both in its being and never-ending becoming.[12]

The Hindu might not speak of Christ as true God and true man. But in Hindu terminology he is like all other men "being as all men are" an eternal and timeless being in a specific psycho-somatic

---

[10]Zaehner, At Sundry Times, p. 194.

[11]Zaehner, Evolution in Religion, pp. 71-72.

[12]Ibid., p. 77.

organism. Christ's death on the cross would then symbolize the death of the whole psychosomatic being which is, strictly speaking, the "not self." His resurrection would symbolize the emergence of the pure Atman from its mortal shell. The Hindu might accept this symbolism. Zaehner, however, feels that as true as the symbolism is, it concerns itself only with individual salvation. Not only the ego but the Atman too must die. To accept the death resurrection of Christ is ultimately to concern oneself with communal salvation.[13]

Zaehner approaches Christ's role in universal salvation by analyzing the "Fall." Part of the original sin of Adam was his ascent to self-consciousness which resulted in the increased differentiation of one human being from another--the Spirit's assertion of its independence from the negative and purely mechanistic aspect of matter. In order to survive, however, man had to become a social animal, and any society needs a center. In ancient societies the center appeared as the King. At times the strongest ego was bound to emerge as the master and subdue all other egos to itself, thereby becoming the center on which all others had necessarily to converge. Time and again the center proved incapable of maintaining itself.

In the Incarnation though, Zaehner sees a significant change. Now the Holy Spirit, diffused throughout the universe, becomes concentrated in a single point. If mankind is to be brought together again, then the process must start with one man who will bring together what has been scattered abroad. This will be done not by force but by sheer attraction. Jesus is the Logos: the principle of rationality manifesting itself in Nature as regularity, order, law, consistence, and coherence. Jesus, the Logos, supplies to the human race the coherence it had lost.[14]

The specific saving function of Christ is

---

[13]Ibid., p. 106.

[14]R. C. Zaehner, <u>Dialectical Christianity and Christian Materialism</u> (London: Oxford University Press, 1971), pp. 84-91.

that of a healer of separation. The Fall of man resulted in three separations: the separation of Adam,
the All-man from God, the separation of each man
from his fellow, and the separation of body from
soul. These separations are healed by the fact that
Christ is the cornerstone which the builders rejected; as such he is the nucleus and foundation
around and on which the new Adam, the new All-man
must be built. Original sin led to the disintegra-
tion of the human race and salvation could no longer
be thought of one single human mass united by a common purpose and a common mode of thought. Christ
came as a second Adam to integrate what had been dis-
persed. He came as one no different from us except
that he was sinless and was also God. Being without sin he was without separation, a unity in him-
self--God and man--and man in the fullest sense with
mind and body immortal spirit. And not only was he
one and whole, integrated within himself, he was
also the bond of union that was to draw all men
together into his own body which is the church. His
mission was not only to reunite man with God, but
to heal the lesion between soul and body in individual man, and to build them into the integrated
whole which is the church.[15]

        The total sacrifice, the total emptying of
everything, both human and divine, constituted the
new birth, the transformation of the man Jesus into
the new all-man Christ, the second Adam. The difference between the two is that whereas self-
consciousness in the first Adam led to the separation and scattering of the human race and to the
loss of that primitive co-consciousness that had
held the race together, the death and resurrection
of Jesus is at the same time the birth of the new
all-man whose body is both sacrament and church. He
is both the innermost and deathless center of every
individual, the visible and tangible bread and wine
which is his body and blood, and the exterior reality which is the Catholic Church.[16]

        3) Christians when they study Indian

─────────────────────────

        [15]R. C. Zaehner, Matter and Spirit (New York:
Harper & Row, 1963), p. 194.

        [16]Zaehner, Evolution in Religion, p. 77.

40

mysticism are frequently surprised that neither in
the Upanishads, nor in the Samkhya Yoga, nor yet in
early Buddhism, is there any emphasis on love.
Zaehner feels that this is understandable given
their view of man's nature and destiny. Without
divine intervention and divine revelation man can
go no further than to realize the timeless wonder
of his own soul. Such a revelation was granted to
the Hindus in the Bhagavad-Gita and to the saints
of southern India, who, while freely recognizing
the marvelous beauty and indestructibility of this
transcendent soul or self, knew that it was even so
dependent on God, and that God, who was its author,
loved it as a father loves his child. This doctrine
which is central to Christianity, struck the Indian
mind with the full force of revelation for it flatly
contradicted the whole idea of detachment that was
the essence of the teaching of the Buddha, the
Sankhya-Yoga and much of the Upanishads.[17]

Hinduism, in the Bhagavad-Gita, had turned
away from the ideal of an impersonal absolute and
in the person of Krishna had embraced a personal God
of love with whom communion and union were possible.
And in the Passion of Christ God shows just what
this love means. It means to give up everything of
yourself without residue or remainder not only for
friends but also for enemies. Here at last the
shell of man's individual consciousness breaks open
to let in the flood of God's love and, through God,
the love of man, his image.

Zaehner asks: Can it be by accident that
the Gita, a brief episode in a lengthy epic has won
universal acceptance in India as perhaps the greatest of all the scriptures? Or are we not rather
bound to see the mysterious workings of the Holy
Spirit preparing us for God's historical Incarnation
in Jesus Christ?[18]

Jesus places heavy emphasis on the command
to love God and neighbor. The love of neighbor is
not easy for the bulk of mystics of all religions;
their prayer turns them toward God to the exclusion

---

[17]Zaehner, Christianity and Other Religions,
pp. 140-41.

[18]Ibid., p. 141.

41

of all else. It is not a question of benevolence
but of the positive love commanded by the New Testament. Even the followers of Christ have difficulty
in implementing this love. But this should not be
surprising since evolutionary progress which means
ever-increasing union in ever-increasing complexity
is a work of love, a love that unites. Then this
union will not be achieved without strife and suffering. Zaehner points to a Christian mystic, Teilhard
de Chardin, as an example of one who had difficulty
in loving the other. As Teilhard says: "The very
idea of entering into spiritual communion with one
who lives independently of me in a universe
apparently closed to mine is disgusting." Why does
he feel so? Christ the connecting link is not felt
to be present.[19]

Other people do not fit into the beatific
experience simply because they are "centers" or
microcosms of their own and as such cannot naturally
combine with a center (another person) that is foreign to them. There must be, Teilhard thought, a
supreme Center of centers on to which all individual
centers must some day converge. So Teilhard con-
ceives of a union of the center of his own personality with the center of all things. This is for him
the cosmic Christ.[20]

So, even the mystic is called upon to see the
Eternal in others. Otherwise, he cannot know Christ
as the center to which all apparently separate centers must aspire, according to Teilhard's theory.
It is only in seeing the Eternal in the other that
one can love the other and then will the mystic's
love of God be complete.[21]

---

[19]Zaehner, Evolution in Religion, p. 44.

[20]Zaehner, Dialectical Christianity and
Christian Materialism, pp. 71-72.

[21]Zaehner, Evolution in Religion, p. 45.
Such an attitude has special importance for the
Christian mystic. "Knowledge of God, to the Christian contemplative too, means primarily assent to
the Christian dogma that God is Absolute Being,
Omniscient Wisdom, and Indefectible Love; it is the
necessary assumption which makes the love of God not
only possible but supremely worthwhile. Such an

Chapter five will examine the probative
value of Zaehner's insights. In particular the fulfillment approach to inter-religious dialogue will
be examined and questioned. Is Christ really a
fulfillment? Has Zaehner chosen only certain points
of comparison? Is the fulfillment model still a
viable means of dialogue? Or do we have to try
newer, less offensive approaches? The question of
Christ as center will be questioned especially from
the viewpoint of its acceptance by non-Christian
religions. The question of universal love proposed
by Zaehner needs criticism from the viewpoint of its
Western presuppositions.

The Incarnation's Influence on the Union of Matter and Spirit

There is another reason why Zaehner under-
lines the importance of Christ's Incarnation. It
is because of the Incarnation's influence on the
union of matter and spirit. Through the coming of
Christ matter, and ultimately man, has been influenced and changed by the Spirit of God acting in
Christ.

This influence can be seen from three basic
viewpoints. 1) First of all, Christ is the Reconciler of the rift between matter and spirit, between
the temporal and the eternal, between God and man.
2) Secondly, in comparison with certain other religions' view of matter, the Christian Incarnation
adds a necessary corrective. 3) Thirdly, the Christian resurrection gives added insight to the meaning
of the body, now and in the hereafter.

1) From the Christian viewpoint the reconciliation of the separation of matter and spirit
comes about by the fact that the Word was made flesh.

This astonishing phrase means nothing less
than that the word of God who also is God and

---

assumption has no claim to validity except in so far
as it was revealed in the teaching and person of
Jesus Christ, Who, according to the Christian scriptures, claimed to be God." Zaehner, Mysticism Sacred
and Profane, p. 177.

therefore pure spirit clothed himself in living matter and thereby united himself indissolubly not only with the human race but with the whole universe of matter which from the very beginning had been in travail with human life and human thought. It is true that from the moment that the Spirit of God moved upon the face of the waters, matter and spirit were locked in close embrace, but with the Incarnation of the Word of God as man, man's own roots in matter, which Indian and other forms of asceticism had so sedulously and so successfully sought to sever, were triumphantly reaffirmed. Matter henceforth was not to be regarded as a drag upon the human spirit, but rather as the indispensable vehicle through which the spirit must work.[22]

The Incarnation has also produced reconciliation between the temporal and the eternal. Thus Zaehner writes:

The Word became flesh. Spirit became matter. In China they had never been separated, but in India and in the West among the Platonists Spirit had ever more imperiously demanded to be separated from matter. God could have followed a policy of non-intervention, but this was not his way. God must become man if man were ever to participate in God's own nature. The eternal must enter the temporal, in what we call history, if man were to regain his lost self and be restored to his father. It is easy to deny the eternal and apparently at least, more noble no doubt to be a Buddhist, but to be a Christian you must be both a Marxist and a Buddhist, both Confucian and Taoist, for in Christ all that has abiding value meets. . . . Through the Incarnation the temporal is raised to the status of the eternal, and the eternal in turn is enmeshed and suffused in the temporal. To deny the marriage of matter and spirit is to be less than a Christian.[23]

This kind of a statement is important for

---

[22] Zaehner, _Matter and Spirit_, pp. 157-58.

[23] Zaehner, _Concordant Discord_, p. 360.

Zaehner for he repeats it in several of his writings. "God becomes man that man may become God." This is the ultimate union of the eternal and the temporal. So Zaehner emphasizes that Christ is God and man, Son of God and Second Adam. Because He is God and man He brings a whole new dimension to man. Through Christ man has the chance and destiny of being built back into the very substance of God. The Spirit had been with man from the Creation, but now man is given the Son. Man not only restores and rebuilds the image of God that was shattered by the Fall. He is also given the privilege of building up the trinitarian life of God in time. Incorporated into the Son, man is called to the Father who is man's beginning and his end.[24]

From another point of view, Christ is also a reconciler because He heals the rift between God and man produced by the Fall of Adam. The impulse of the Spirit at Creation was to bring man and matter toward ever closer cohesion and unity. Through the misuse of his consciousness man reversed and inhibited this impulse of the Spirit. So a second entrance of the divine into matter was necessary. Thus, the second person of the Christian Trinity, the rational principle of the universe, took on the form of matter in its most complex and highly organized state, i.e., the form of thinking and self-conscious man.[25]

Christ's mission was to bring together all things that had been separated by sin. This he does by making the human being whole in himself, by reconciling man to God, and by sanctifying man and through man all the material world. Buddha came to deliver spirit from the toils of matter. Christ came to close the gap between matter and spirit caused by original sin. Matter was to be pressed into the service of spirit so that the harmony of the universe might be restored. This harmony would be restored on a morally responsible plane in which the virtues of human-heartedness, righteousness, decorum and wisdom could flourish in the light of the

---

[24]Zaehner, Matter and Spirit, p. 192.

[25]Ibid., p. 199.

45

Holy Spirit, the giver of life who is at the same time love.[26]

2) Zaehner next, compares the Incarnation's unifying action on matter and spirit with similar Hindu and Buddhist views. The latter views he finds deficient owing mainly to an inadequate appreciation of matter. He feels that they lead one to embrace an extreme view: either the changeless peace of pure spirit or the ever changing turmoil of matter. And either of these views denies one's status as a full human being existing here and now in time.[27] On the other hand, the glorification of matter, the acceptance of flesh and the world is to accept the obvious meaning of the Incarnation. The following comparisons then, are used by Zaehner to emphasize the importance of the religious value of matter.

In an article entitled "Dogma" Zaehner examines the religious presuppositions separating different religions and in particular concerning the nature of God. For him it is an issue between theism on the one hand and either monism or pantheism on the other. Are we ourselves God or is he something or somebody other than ourselves? On this subject, Zaehner says, we must choose for we cannot logically cling to both views. The question is then examined with particular reference to Hindu belief with Zaehner concluding that Hindu belief has not chosen. Rather they have combined an intense devotion to a personal God with a purely monist philosophy.

> It is a great tribute to the religious genius of the Indian people that they have developed one of the most beautiful devotional literatures of the world yet they are hampered by monistic dogmas which make nonsense of prayer and devotion. If forced to give an opinion on this extremely tricky subject, I should say that, without trying to go into the very involved question of the validity of one set of dogmas as

---

[26]Zaehner, _Christianity and Other Religions_, p. 146.

[27]Zaehner, _Dialectical Christianity and Christian Materialism_, p. 4.

46

against another, the dogma of the monist must
militate against devotion to a personal God if
(as the great Vaisnava Puranas point out) that
God, as displayed in his incarnations, is really
illusory.[28]

Zaehner then proceeds to contrast this attitude with the Christian attitude, pointing out that
Christianity offers an opposite extreme. Both God,
the Creator and the created universe are real: between them is a real separation. To heal this
separation God did become incarnate in Christ,
thereby bringing man back, soul and body, into the
divine order. God and man meet really and wholly
in the person of Christ. The point of the Incarnation is the sanctification of the body, and through
it, of the whole matter. "I would be the last to
claim that the christian dogma is any less unreason-
able than the TAT TUAM ASI formula. I say that it
restores to man the unity of his being which the
dualist systems and the monistic mystics seek to
deny. Of course, neither dogma can, of its very
nature be proved."[29]

Another way of looking at this is to say
that matter cannot be ignored. We all know about
the prison of matter but the Cross of Christ and his
descent into hell teach us that there is a prison
of the spirit too, the prison of absolute Kaivalyam
of absolute "isolation," what the Sufis call tafrid.
To be truly alive and eternally alive, then, man
must die a second death and be born again in matter
of some kind. Zaehner suspects that this is what
the Hindus mean by "the subtle body," of which the
resurrected body of Christ is the prototype. Atman
must be re-united with buddhi so that it can again
become conscious--realize itself as the "cit" as
well as the "sat" in the Trinity of Sac-cid-ananda.
To realize oneself simply as Sat is to waste away
in the spirit to which one restricts oneself and to
die of inanition.[30]

The GITA is the middle way between the

---

[28]Zaehner, "Dogma," pp. 17-18.

[29]Ibid., p. 18.

[30]Zaehner, Evolution in Religion, p. 109.

absolute monism of the non-dualist Vedanta and the
absolute dualism of the Sankhya. In effect, absolute monism is in practice identical with the
absolute dualism of both Sankhya and Theravada Buddhism in that it sees salvation solely in terms of
spirit. Matter, whether it is regarded as being
merely illusory or having an independent existence
of its own is that which enslaves spirit. Matter
and spirit cannot be brought together unless spirit
enters deeply into matter and moulds it towards a
higher and more unified form of existence. This is
what the Gita does, and in this it supplements and
completes Christianity.[31]

Nevertheless, in the Gita, Krishna starts
from the basic assumption that this world must be
renounced. In the New Testament Christ takes upon
himself the sufferings of this world and makes them
his own. He shows that life is serious. It is not
the sport of an irresponsible God (Krishna or Rama)
nor is it a meaningless flux as it is for the
Buddha. This is the unbridgeable gulf that separates traditional Christianity from traditional
Buddhism. Christ becomes man so that he may make
all mankind his own, and beyond mankind all the
world of matter.

Thus, Christ is not the Buddha, for by his
Incarnation he sanctifies matter and promises us
not Nirvana, but eternal life. "And without matter
of some sort I do not understand how there can be
life."[32] Nirvana is the extinction of life and
therefore of all the vareity that is inseparable
from life: it is "something with which there is no
commerce, impalpable, devoid of distinguishing mark,
unthinkable, indescribable, its essence the firm
conviction of the oneness of itself, bringing all
development to an end, tranquil and mild, devoid of
duality" (Mandukya Upanishad). This, For Zaehner,
is the very opposite of the eternal life which is
the good news of the Incarnation and Resurrection.
The resurrection is in his view the fertilization
of Nirvana and the sanctification of matter itself.
But unless we accept the Buddha's message of selflessness and self-denial, we cannot share in

[31]Ibid., pp. 69-70.

[32]Zaehner, Concordant Discord, p. 357.

48

Christ's resurrected life. By the same token, unless we accept matter and the body we cannot accept the resurrection.

3) Zaehner's third point concerns the future life. If man is to live it must be the whole man who lives, not just part of him, i.e., his soul. To view the body as the dark prison of the luminous soul is inadequate and as we have seen, contrary to Christ's joining of Spirit and Matter. Rather, the resurrection of Jesus is a sanctification of the body itself, a promise that man too will be resurrected and transformed from a physical body to what St. Paul called a "spiritual body" or what the Hindus would call a "subtle body." This transformation is not a final separation of spirit from matter, since salvation is a making whole. It is the resurrection of the whole man, in body and soul. This is not the survival of the purely physical body, nor rebirth in a new physical body; as would be the case for reincarnation. It is the spiritual body glorified by all the good it has done on earth.

In Zaehner's view Indian religion suffers from incompleteness on this point. Its rejection of the phenomenal world either as an illusion or as a prison of the immortal spirit has to lead to some dissatisfaction. Modern Hindu writers like Sri Aurobindo, Hiriyanna, and Radhakrishnan have felt this acutely. It is open to doubt, at the very least, whether they would ever have felt it had not they been faced with the Christian challenge that this world is a testing ground in which man works out the quality of his own immortality. The importance of this world is best seen in the basis of Christian faith: the resurrection of the body of Christ Jesus from the dead. This is not just a question of the immortality of the soul. Rather, the resurrection of the body distinguishes Christianity most sharply from all other Gnostic religions, whether of Mediterranean or Indian origin, which see the body as the prison of the soul.[33]

---

[33]Zaehner, At Sundry Times, p. 168. Zaehner also notes elsewhere that this criticism is not without foundation. "Now it has been a fairly constant criticism of both Hinduism and Buddhism from the Christian side that both are wholly other-worldly and pay all too little attention to what

So, Zaehner rejects a pantheism of nature
which the pantheist will mistake for God. He also
rejects a mystical extreme which would reject matter
in favour of the bliss of a timeless state of being
which the Buddhists call Nirvana. Both of these
attitudes are perversions since it is the function
of Spirit to perfect matter and to transform it
into itself, each working for the good of the other.
This is the purpose of the Incarnation, but the Incarnation is only the beginning of a spiritual
regeneration of the whole of creation whose fulfillment is most likely reserved for a far distant
future. For, Christ, in his Incarnation, crucifixion, resurrection and ascension, did not save
the world, but only showed the way through which
the world might be saved. Of itself matter cannot
be saved--it cannot rise above its inherent muta-
bility and propensity to decay until it has given
birth to spirit. This process of birth, seen from
the viewpoint of evolutionary time, may take millions of years.[34]

The final chapter will have to evaluate
Zaehner's claims. His remarks on the "religious"
value of matter give an insight which contemporary
Eastern religious studies recognize. But once again
the question remains as to his Western presuppositions concerning matter and spirit as well as
presuppositions concerning Christ's resurrection.

A Comparison of Christ and Other Religious Figures

Zaehner also sees a superiority of Christ
when he compares Christ and certain other religious

---

goes on in this world. There is no doubt that this
criticism has gone home and that the reform Hinduism
of the last two centuries has tried to remedy this
defect, if indeed defect it be. Again it has been
to the Gita that the Hindu reformers have turned,
reinterpreting it in a more activist sense." Concordant Discord, p. 108.

[34]Zaehner, Dialectical Christianity and
Christian Materialism, p. 8.

figures. It is a superiority that is not meant as triumphalism. Rather Zaehner once again is working from a fulfillment theme or preparation theme. The comparisons are not worked out in a detailed way, in fact, sometimes they are only made as part of a broader evaluation. Still they offer some insight and illustrate Zaehner's method.

1) As we have already seen Zaehner proposes Christ as a fulfillment of certain religious aspirations of men of other religions. This is true with regard to Hinduism for Zaehner views Hinduism as a preparation for the gospel, a gospel which will complete and perfect Hindu teaching. This was his stance in his early writings. It continued into the late 1960s in his Giffort lectures: "For while I am willing to concede that, if the central doctrine of Christianity is that God becomes man in order that man may become God, then Hinduism can be seen as very much more of a praeparatio Evangelica than can the Old Testament for which such an idea is blasphemous."[35]

So Hinduism does prepare one to accept Christ's Incarnation. But Zaehner also notes that the various Avatars of Vishnu are not really comparable to the Christian doctrine of the Incarnation. Nobody would seriously maintain that Rama and Krishna were historical characters. Of course, this fact does not impress the Hindu. For him the phenomenal world is simply the Lila or sport of the deity and has no real existence in itself. The incarnations of Vishnu too occurring as they do in the phenomenal world, are equally illusory.[36]

Even the purpose of the incarnations of Vishnu differs from the Christian idea of Incarnation. Christ becomes incarnate in order to vanquish sin and restore the relationship between God and man which had been severed by Adam's sin. Christ's incarnation is unique; He is sole mediator. The Kingdom of God founded in time on this earth will be subsumed by the Kingdom of God in Heaven at the end of time. Life progresses to a final redemption at

---

[35]Zaehner, Concordant Discord, p. 15.

[36]Ibid., pp. 439-40.

the end of time when body and soul will share immortality and life everlasting. On the other hand, for the Hindu, as we have already noted, there is no progress in time: time is cyclical being bound to endless repetitive cycles emanating from and being absorbed into the matrix of being. In such a scheme of things, which the Bhagavad-Gita accepts, Vishnu's incarnation is not overly important. His incarnation as Krishna, however, promises deliverance from reincarnation not only in this world-era, but also in all world-eras. He calls upon man to share eternally in the life of God.[37]

Hinduism is mystical through and through, and the radical reversal of the dominant trend in the Bhagavad-Gita is, therefore, of overriding importance for it smashes the wall of elaborate self-sufficiency that fallen man had built around himself and brings him face to face with God. Both Taoism, Buddhism, and the Samkhya-Yoga are religions that opt out of life, reject the world by rejecting individuality and the responsibilities that individuality brings with it. Krishna comes to change all that, for he implies that though, theoretically, there may be nothing wrong in this, it really amounts to a colossal act of spiritual pride, for it means that man, by seeking to be like God in his eternal impassability and unfathomable peace, spurns to be like God in his capacity of creator and sustainer of the world. This is the acme of hybris; for if God is not too proud to keep the world in being, who is man to turn his back on it?[38]

In addition, the quality of these incarnate figures varies. Christ became man that he might show forth the true nature of God. The God he reveals is the transcendent Creator and also the suffering servant. In the Indian tradition both Rama and Krishna prefigure Christ. Krishna in the Bhagavad-Gita reveals the love of God for man. Rama is prepared to divest himself of his royalty and lead a beggar's life. And yet neither is quite satisfactory as an incarnation of God, for they lack

---

[37]Zaehner, At Sundry Times, p. 117.

[38]Zaehner, Matter and Spirit, p. 119.

all ultimate seriousness. Rama, for example, gives up a kingdom to satisfy the spiteful whim of a spoilt queen. At times he tends to stiffness and a respectability which is a bore. Krishna, outside the Gita, is a trickster, the author of foul play, a wanton lover, and too frivolous to be taken seriously outside India. Unless one ignores Christ, he must be taken seriously.[39]

Actually Zaehner goes beyond Krishna or Rama, declaring that the Hindu figure Yudhishthira, the King of Righteousness, is the figure of Christ among the Hindus. In the face of evil this king does not rail against God; he condemned a social system that glorified senseless war. He is a figure of outraged compassion. He is a servant of the servants of God. Yudhishthira is meek, and loses all that is dear to him because he was ready to lay down his life for his friends. He is a Christ figure, but Yudhishthira was not God nor did he claim to be God.[40]

Zaehner also feels that Christ fulfills the Bodhisattva ideal. The Bodhisattva ideal is perhaps the most grandiose that the Indian mind has ever conceived. It finds its fulfillment as nowhere else in the figure of the crucified. But whereas the Bodhisattvas are mythical beings thought out by man in his desperate longing that such beings might exist, Christ is the true Bodhisattva, God made man, suffering with man, and crucified by man and for man that He might release him--not indeed from the suffering of this world, but from the burden of sin that causes that suffering. "When the Bodhisattva's work is done he disappears. Christ, however, does not disappear. On the third day he arises again in

---

[39]Zaehner, Concordant Discord, p. 355. And elsewhere he adds emphasis to the fulfillment theme. "For Christians too, Krishna, the incarnate God of love, who is yet rex tremendae majestatis, prefigures, as no other mythological figure can, the historical person of Jesus Christ, the Word made man who will yet return to pass judgment on mankind." Matter and Spirit, p. 119.

[40]Zaehner, Concordant Discord, p. 355.

body and in soul, a whole man who is also God. . . .
And as he rose from the dead so shall all men rise
from the dead. Christ's resurrection is the
earnest of all men's resurrection."[41]

2) In considering Guatma, the Buddha,
Zaehner in no way underestimates his goodness. On
the contrary, he extols the Buddha's virtue and the
holiness of his "way." But there is some difficulty
with some of his teachings and attitudes which
Zaehner sees as deficient.

As we have already seen, a basic problem is
the attitude towards the world. Christ came into
the world to be the world, to be with the world,
and to suffer with the world. The Buddha came into
the world of un-ease, and suffering, and flux to
save us from the world. Ultimately, says Zaehner,
the way of the Buddha denies our total humanity and
our specific status in the order of creation as men
here and now. The Buddha's teaching leads one into
a "trackless" and "untraceable" form of existence.
Christ's teaching leads to eternal life, indeed
sharing the life of the risen Christ in body and
soul. The two views of salvation correspond to the
two views on the nature of man, life and death.
Whereas the Christian would not deny the validity of
the Hindu or Buddhist experience of the eternity
of the human soul which they call Nirvana, he would
deny that this represents man's ultimate bliss. As
the Hindu theists themselves, who reacted against
Sankara's rigid monism, realized, the soul's realization of its own timelessness and isolation is not
the final purpose of human existence. Rather it is
the soul's union and communion with God and its re-
union with a transfigured body.[42]

In their very different ways the Buddha's
Enlightenment and Christ's Resurrection guarantee
immortality in some sense. There is of course an
enormous difference between them. The Buddha's
Enlightenment means that he has freed himself from
everything that could possibly attach him to the
world of Samsara. The whole process of samsara

---

[41]Zaehner, At Sundry Times, p. 187.

[42]Zaehner, The Concise Encyclopedia of Living
Faiths, p. 416.

came to an end though he still lived; it is the total cessation of becoming which is Nirvana. Whatever the Resurrection of Christ means, it does not mean this: it does not mean the negation of becoming in that which does not become. It means rather the assumption and transformation of the transient into the "unborn, not become, not made, uncompounded."[43]

Zaehner also thinks that there is a significant contrast between the crucifixion of Christ and the Buddhist concept of Nirvana. The crucifixion of Christ means the total giving of self: translated into Indian terms this means giving up the "ego" and the love of possessions. It also means the crucifixion of the eternal essence which is the very ground of the soul and a final refusal to accept a timeless beatitude apart from God. Zaehner claims that one should be led to die to desiring an immortal essence which claims identity with God and which claims to need nothing or no one. Such an attitude leads one to no longer care about the world or mankind.

It is this, the ultimate selfishness of a solitary Nirvana, the more selfish because it believes itself to be selfless, that is crucified with Christ on the Cross. It is the symbolic abrogation of the Hinayana or "defective vehicle" of the Buddhists and the inauguration of the Mahayana or "great vehicle" in a real historical setting. For the Mahayanists saw that the old idea of the Arhant who abandons the world to sink himself into a featureless Nirvana was radically selfish and a betrayal of the Buddha's own compassion, for the Buddha himself had refused to abandon the world until he had fully expounded his message of salvation. Yet the Mahayana too had its weaknesses, for its Bodhisattvas are all purely mythological beings and its Nirvana is a void of positive content as is the older one. Christ, on the other hand, is the historical Bodhisattva, and the "Nirvana" he offers includes both union with God through him and communion with all men in and through his mystical body.[44]

---

[43] Zaehner, Concordant Discord, p. 103.

[44] Zaehner, Matter and Spirit, p. 198.

3) When Zaehner examines Islam he does so
with great respect for the religious intensity of
the Muslim tradition. He accepts Muhammad as a true
prophet sent by God as well as he acknowledges the
credentials of Islam both as an historical and a
biblical religion, i.e., "of the book," viz. Quran.
It is to the Quran, and not to Mumammad, that Zaehner
turns for a comparison with Christ. This would agree
with the observation of Charles Davis: "It is a mistake to suppose the Muhammad stands to Islam as
Jesus Christ stands to Christianity. . . . The place
occupied by Christ in the Christian religion belongs
in Islam to the Quran as the very word of God. Muhammad's position is roughly parallel to that of
Paul or the Apostles."[45]

The place of Christ in the comparison is
stated quite clearly:

> As against Islam Christianity would seem to
> have only one really effective argument, and
> that is that Jesus Christ, was God incarnate
> and claimed to be the "Son of God." If this
> is so, His word and its continuation in the
> church He founded must take precedence over
> any merely prophetic revelation. The Muham-
> madan answer to this is, of course, that Jesus
> never made any such claim and that Christians had
> falsified His message.[46]

Zaehner argues that the Quran, as opposed to
traditional Muslim orthodoxy, does not explicitly
deny any specific Christian doctrine except that
Christ is the son of God. The latter doctrine was
denied because it was thought to imply physical
procreation by God which is unthinkable in One who
is pure Spirit. The argumentation goes further to
show that the Quran does not deny the Trinity, the
Atonement, the Crucifixion, or the Resurrection and
further that one can find traces of these doctrines
in the Quran.[47] "Thus it appears from a careful

---

[45]Charles Davis, Christ and the World Religions (New York: Herder and Herder, 1971), p. 104.

[46]Zaehner, At Sundry Times, pp. 196-97.

[47]Ibid., pp. 195-217. Ten years later
Zaehner was to modify this argumentation: "Whether

reading of the Quran itself that the gap between Christianity and Islam as it is first announced in the Quran is very much narrower than the gap between Orthodox Christianity and the tradition of Orthodox Islam. There is the possibility of dialogue and therefore the possibility of understanding."[48]

The latter sentence shows a basic approach of Zaehner. The obstacle to accepting Christ is less between Christ and the Quran than between Christ and the Islamic orthodox tradition. Zaehner tries to show that this tradition has at times not been faithful to or has misinterpreted the Quran. The Quran gives evidence that Jesus is greater indeed than Muhammad who never claimed to be more than a man. Jesus is the Messiah, the Word of God, the Word of Truth, a Spirit from God, the Spirit of God.[49] The Quran would appear to accept Christ's divinity as the word of Truth, while laying great stress on His humanity. Of course, Muslims deny the divinity of Christ.

But there still is a gap and an insoluble problem. From the Christian viewpoint the problem is accepting a prophetic message, some six hundred years after the Incarnation of Christ, which denied or ignored the redemptive mission of Christ. The problem is compounded by a lack of newness in Muhammad's message as well as a lack of the mystical element in his teaching. Christianity is a prophetic religion, but one which fulfilled the previous Semitic Old Covenant by introducing into it a mystical element which it has in common with the religions of Asia, but which is absent from the other semitic religions.

Muhammad, in the Quran, nowhere denies and

---

there is any way of reconciling the Jesus of the Koran with the Jesus of the Gospel I have already discussed in a previous book (viz. At Sundry Times). My arguments were ingenious: I no longer quite believe them." Concordant Discord, p. 30.

[48]Zaehner, Christianity and Other Religions, p. 107.

[49]Ibid., p. 103.

sometimes affirms specifically Christian beliefs, and so far as his sublime conception of the unity and transcendence of God is affirmed, he may justly claim to be "the seal of the Prophets." He adds nothing new to what has been previously revealed because he is a prophet, and no more than a prophet. The mystical bond of love which Christ, in His own Person, brings to fill out the hopes of the prophets before Him is lacking in the one Prophet who came after Him.[30]

The comparisons once again indicate Zaehner's attitude concerning the uniqueness of Christ. They are more illustrative rather than probative or exhaustive, as the final chapter will indicate. Outside of the Christian faith context they have a limited value. The sublimity of Christ's person and teaching offer a true challenge to all religious men. But it is important to note that one is challenged not compelled.

---

[50]Zaehner, At Sundry Times, p. 216.

58

CHAPTER III

ZAEHNER'S VIEW OF THE CHURCH. THE UNIVERSAL

MIND OF CHRIST AS PRESENT IN THE FAITH

AND UNITY OF THE CHRISTIAN CHURCH

The Church as a Center of Unity

Zaehner's view of the Church flows from his understanding of Christ. The Church is seen as the extension of the risen Christ living in time and space. On the one hand Zaehner's imagery is based on a Pauline understanding of the body of Christ and the Communion of Saints. On the other hand his understanding of the Church is greatly influenced by Teilhard de Chardin who described the Church in evolutionary terms. Thus, we have Zaehner's appreciation of the original church, the church as it is presently, and the church as it will be, or ought to be. The latter aspect is particularly influenced by Teilhard resulting in a visionary view of the church. This leads to tension between a theoretical and a practical view of the Church. In the dialogue between world religions arguments concerning a visionary, theoretical church have a limited value. But there is value since the dialogue is not limited to the present moment only.

It should also be noted that some of Zaehner's writing concerning the church originate in an admittedly subjective conviction. At times his work is a subjective interpretation of the religious history of man seen from an individual angle within the overall structure of the Catholic Church. This, he claims, is not simply bias; it is the way he has come to see things after much study. His view does not presuppose a superiority of Christianity. It simply follows, in his eyes, from what has been said previously about Christ, who, says Zaehner,

59

inaugurated and now vivifies the Church.

Because of the church's dependence on Christ much of the reasoning and method in chapter two is bound to reappear in this chapter. Thus, a) the Church too is a center of unity for all mankind considered both individually and collectively. Mankind's movement is one of convergence upon a center which is Christ-Church. This convergence will ultimately enable man to overcome his isolation and grow into greater solidarity. b) Zaehner also feels that the Church alone is universal enough in its appeal to allow man to fully achieve himself and achieve communion with his fellow man. Hinduism, Buddhism, and Marxism, unlike the Church, lack an integrating center. c) The fulfillment model is also applied to the Church which is a via media between varying religious aspirations of men. In particular the Church provides a balance between the desire for universal and individual salvation as well as between the prophetic and mystical traditions of world religions. d) The Eucharist is a symbol of the unity achieved by Christ and his Church. e) Zaehner's realism leads him to criticize the church as it now exists. The church leaves much to be desired as a practically effective center of human solidarity.

Certain key points are threaded throughout this chapter some of which appeared in chapter two: unity; convergence in a center; universality; individual and corporate salvation; fulfillment of religious aspirations. The emphasis shows their centrality to Zaehner's thought. The first to be treated in this chapter is unity.

For Zaehner the essence of Catholicism is unity.[1] The principle of unity, based on Christ, is one of the unique factors of the Church, corresponding to a deep craving in man for unity. It might be best characterized, as Zaehner sees it, as a biblical, evolutionary unity. It is biblical inasmuch as the insight is based on the unifying action of Christ and his Church as interpreted by the Christian scriptures. The unity is evolutionary since, as Teilhard de Chardin saw and Zaehner maintains, it is an on-going process yet to be achieved fully.

---

[1]R. C. Zaehner, Matter and Spirit (New York: Harper & Row, 1963), p. 22.

60

From a biblical point of view Zaehner presents Christ as the "Second Adam" the new "All-Man" who, in rectifying the fall of Adam, starts the trend towards moulding humanity into unity. Adam sinned through pride and self-conceit, and the human race degenerated into separate and divided cultures and individuals, each despising his neighbor. But, when Christ had achieved his task and demonstrated the totality of God's love for man on the cross, had risen, and ascended into heaven, he sent the Spirit, that impelled the infant church on its way--the Church that is itself the material as well as the mystical body of the risen Lord.[2]

The unifying action of humanity takes place, then, in the one body of the Church whose head is Christ. The imagery comes directly from St. Paul especially from his letter to the Corinthians (1 Cor. 12:12-27). Through Christ and his Church the human race is destined to grow together until everything is subjected to him (1 Cor. 15). The very consummation of the whole human race through the God-man into God was God's purpose from the beginning (Eph. 1:9-10). The main variation from the body of Christ image occurs when Zaehner switches to the "spouse" theme.

Zaehner's reading of the Pentecost event leads him to the conclusion that the history of the Church has to be seen in evolutionary terms. The miracle of Pentecost reversed the tide of evolution itself, for from this moment it could be seen that the Church's destiny was to rebuild mankind in the image and unity of Christ. The scattering of the nations represented by the Tower of Babel was annulled. The convergence of humanity upon itself had already begun. The Church of Christ was born and the symbol of unity and union was found.[3]

Pentecost was the promise, not the adult fulfillment of what we call the Communion of Saints. The church has the guarantee but not yet the fulfillment. The church, as the body of Christ, is a living organism subject always to sin. And the root-cause of sin is a collective egoism which is put in the place of the free working of the Holy Spirit. But

---

[2]Ibid., p. 202.   [3]Ibid., p. 195.

it is the Holy Spirit who is the universal spirit
giving life to all religions whether Semitic, Indian,
or Chinese. It is the Holy Spirit in Christianity
says Zaehner, re-appearing as the Ruhu'l-qudus in
the Koran; it is the Prana of the Upanishads and
the drive of evolution. But always and everywhere
it is thwarted by man's efforts to find a fixed,
still state of Brahman, in a world that is irre-
mediably in flux.[4] The thwarting of the Spirit's
work of unification will perhaps continue, in
Zaehner's view for hundreds or even thousands of
years.

Based on the scriptural insight Zaehner concludes that a process of convergence is at work both
in individual man and the community of man: what he
calls "solitary" and "solidary." The convergence
takes place in Christ and his church. This is a
re-affirmation of the Catholic ideal being first
and foremost unity--unity through the Holy Spirit in
Christ for the Father.

The unity of mankind that Zaehner discusses
is actually twofold: unity on the individual level
and in the community. In the individual it means the
gathering up of all the functions into their immortal center, what the Hindus call the "self" and what
Paul called "the life of Christ who lives in me."
In the community it is the church as the Body of
Christ in which each individual has a part to play
in harmony with the whole. This is an ideal. The
church is not just an organization: it is a living
organism in which the part cannot live in separation
from the whole. This is a form of collective mysticism which has never existed and perhaps never will.
It is nevertheless, in Zaehner's opinion, what
Communion of Saints means and is the hidden aspiration of all mankind.[5]

---

[4]Zaehner, Evolution in Religion, p. 79.

[5]Zaehner, Concordant Discord, p. 374. This
has been Zaehner's conviction even from the time of
his earliest writings on comparative religion. He
wrote: "Along with the instinct to preserve himself
man has the instinct to negate himself, a mad longing
to escape from his cramping and confining ego in
which he is forever imprisoned. This instinct was,
of course, recognized in the earliest times in the

Teilhard[6] conceived of a new type of mysticism, that of the mass of mankind converging upon itself and upon God. This is a slow integration of

Christian Church: through the powerful agency of St. Paul the doctrine of the mystical body of the church took shape. Man was no longer left in miserable solitude; he became one with Christ and through Christ with God in the mystical union of the Church of which Christ was the head and individual Christians the members. Individuality is transcended in the greater unity of the Church. Among the Hindus the transcending of the ego was recognized as being the whole purpose of religion. Separate individuality is either merged into the infinite . . . or actually becomes identical with the infinite." R. C. Zaehner, "The Religious Instinct" in The New Outline of Modern Knowledge, ed. A. Pryce-Jones (London: Gollancz Ltd., 1936), p. 71.

[6]As we have seen in chapter two and will see in this chapter much of what Zaehner has to say about Christ-Church is influenced by Teilhard de Chardin's writings. His last five books have been largely influenced by Teilhard. Thus it is surprising to see a rather severe criticism of Teilhard in Zaehner's latest book. "It is no doubt true that the cosmic Christ of the first chapter of Paul's letter to the Colossians . . . has been much neglected by modern Christianity. But to emphasize it at the expense of everything else is quite simply heresy in the literal sense of the word, choosing what suits you at the expense of everything else" (p. 179). "Teilhard's vision of a world converging irreversibly on a cosmic center of centers is based on a prolonged participation in cosmic consciousness. . . . The vision, of course, is nothing more than a vision, but his insistence that evolution must result in man converging on himself runs very much counter to the evidence of our times, is frequently puerile, and makes a mockery of human suffering" (p. 179). "Teilhard is not really interested in human beings as such. What interests him is his pipe dream of humanity converging on itself and never mind the casualties on the way" (p. 180). (Teilhard's insensitivity to suffering seems to bother Zaehner the most and make him question the validity of Teilhard's vision.) "How hollow does Teilhard's talk of the amorizing of the universe

63

the mind of all mankind around its center, Christ, in rational adoration; and this is what is meant by the Communion of Saints. Evolution itself is driving mankind into the convergence in unanimity and thereby to an immortal life that joins not only individual souls to God, but also welds together all the millions of human souls that form the one body of Christ in union and communion with each other. United around one center, says Zaehner, we can look forward in hope to the communion of saints, the co-ordination of all our thinking and hoping and adoration.[7] Christ and Christianity must be seen in and through evolution--from individuality through collectivity to a unity in diversity centered on the cosmic Christ. Thus the Church is an instrument of human unity ready and at hand.

The church then is to be the focal point for both individual and communal unity. Teilhard's vision sees the dovetailing of individual minds into a universal mind, which for Christians, is the Word, or Christ. This vision is much like Engel's own vision of the sum total of human minds, working together in space and time and converging in an infinite mind. Zaehner wonders if something of this is perhaps already with us in the Catholic Church, the unity of whose faith and thought is habitually called the "mind" of the church. "And this is what the church . . . stands for and offers: the

---

sound now. We have failed to love one another and remain isolated as individuals and nations. Why talk of the cosmic Christ when we have been and are deaf to his message? Why talk of convergence through love when we can't even love one another" (p. 182). Zaehner, Drugs, Mysticism, and Make-Believe, p. 210.

[7]Zaehner, Matter and Spirit, pp. 185, 205, 206. And elsewhere: "Chardin had a vision of a new type of Christianity based on evolution and the convergence of the world along the axis of the Roman Catholic Church--for him the only possible axis--towards a cosmic Christ who stood at the end of the road to integrate this widened and now all-comprehensive church back to his sacred heart." Zaehner, Drugs, Mysticism, and Make-Believe, p. 196.

ultimate solidarity of each in all and all in each, an organism of persons in all their variety united around the Person who is the center and the circumference of them all, Christ, and impelled by the Holy Spirit towards encounter with the Father."[8]

According to Teilhard evolution is a progressive spiritualization of matter--from chaos to cosmos, from cosmos to life, from life to simple consciousness, from simple consciousness to self-consciousness, and from self-consciousness to "cosmic consciousness" through which men cease to be closed individuals whose souls are isolated from the Soul of the World. It is a progressive organization of indeterminate matter into ever more complex monads, the highest and most particularized of which is man. The church is the visible symbol of the Soul of the World. So, it is the church which is the point of unity where these closed individuals can overcome their isolation. "In his later work Teilhard de Chardin tended to lose sight of the man Jesus in his vision of the cosmic Christ to whom the Soul of the World is betrothed. The two cannot, however be separated, and the link between them is the Church, the visible symbol of the Soul of the World, the Bride of Christ, not yet saved, but destined to be saved in the last days."[9]

The communion of saints of course might be better characterized as the communion of would-be-saints. A promise was given by Christ to his church even if the reality has not been realized. It is rather an ideal, the ideal of a society as tightly knit together as is a human body, the body of the Man-God Christ Himself, dead and resurrected in the Church he had founded. This was the substance of the Catholic Church and of the Catholic idea--the idea of coherence and totality in one living organism that one day was to embrace the whole world.[10]

The ideal, of course, is far from realized.

---

[8]Zaehner, Matter and Spirit, p. 205.

[9]Zaehner, Dialectical Christianity and Christian Materialism, p. 91.

[10]Zaehner, Evolution in Religion, pp. 87-88.

With the birth of self-consciousness men lost their
sense of solidarity, their ability to interpenetrate
one another in a shared consciousness of the whole.
To regain this sense of solidarity and interpenetra-
tion in a common effort towards God, the point of
cohesion of all things, is how Teilhard sees the
destiny of mankind.

> It is a surging forward and upwards, a soldering
> of multiplicity into unity, an aspiration of mat-
> ter towards spirit, of individuality towards
> totality, of all individual souls, each in its
> way a bride of Christ, towards the universal
> bride of Christ, the soul of the Church--the
> Church as it one day may be, the universal and
> Catholic Church of all mankind. Then the Body
> and Bride will coalesce into a spiritual body
> purified and fit for the final consummation of
> the sacred marriage with the Son of God.[11]

As the world learns to overcome its sin, then
it can grow in peace and understanding into a solidary mankind reconciled to God in Christ and Christ's
body, the Church. Such a unity is too far off to
predict. Nevertheless a new age of co-operation is
upon us. Over a period of hundreds of years perhaps
the church will slowly grow, attracting to herself
all the craving towards unity that lies deep in the
heart of every individual person.

> The Church will proclaim ever more insistently
> the indissoluble marriage of Spirit and matter
> in Christ, and rejecting private attempts at
> personal spiritualization, will appear so soli-
> dary and so centered on her divine Founder that
> all other organizations, because they lack such
> a center, and because they are strangers to a
> sacramental system that nurtures each individual
> . . . must inevitably feel the strange attrac-
> tion she cannot help exercising. She will be
> resisted to the last, but this resistance will
> weaken as humanity converges ever more insistent-
> ly on itself.[12]

---

[11]Zaehner, <u>Concordant Discord</u>, p. 408.

[12]Zaehner, <u>Matter and Spirit</u>, p. 207.

The unity toward which mankind is converging
the Catholic sees already there in embryo in the
material and sacramental structure of the Catholic
Church. How all mankind will ultimately be fitted
into this structure the Catholic would not presume
to say. But he would scarcely be a Catholic at all
if he doubted that this was so. Else he would be
false to him who prayed "that they all may be one."
For the Catholic this unity has never ceased to
exist in the Church. That it will continue to exist
and grow until it embraces within itself all mankind,
he cannot but believe and hope. But it would be
folly to expect the full unity of the church to be
manifest to all so long as the church is not
cleansed from sin: and that will not be till the
end of time.[13]

---

[13]Ibid., p. 18. At times Zaehner refers to
the Catholic Church, at other times to the Christian
Church, and at still other times simply to the
Church. In a personal interview in May 1972, at Oxford, I asked him when it was necessary to distinguish the Catholic and Christian Church. His reply
indicated that the ecumenical movement had produced
such unity of essentials that some Catholics, for
example, no longer knew what distinguished them from
Protestants. Nevertheless, he did mention that:
"The Catholic Church will become the focal point of
all Christians--which obviously is coming." This
does not indicate a mass conversion to the Catholic
Church. Rather, in the re-unification of the Christian Church, the unifying and universal features
which the Catholic Church has maintained, will stand
out as part of the essential features of the renewed
Christian Church. Yet, Zaehner still makes some
sharp distinctions between the sects in his latest
books, maintaining the attitude that the Catholic
Church, at least in theory, is the best embodiment
of what Zaehner envisages as "the Church." ". . .
the 'Church' has never meant to Protestants what it
means to Catholics. This is obvious for the Catholic
ideal has always been unity as its very name implies.
Protestants have always laid more stress on private
judgement which has, of course, led to the prolife-
ration of Protestant sects." In commenting on Bonhoeffer's idea of Church and its division into sects,
Zaehner notes: ". . . and the whole concept of the
Church no longer made sense to him (Bonhoeffer) in
a secularized world. He took Protestantism to its

Even the present dialogue between major world religions indicates a process of convergence, a religious evolution leading to unity.

> Now for the first time the religions of the world confront each other directly, and it is to be assumed that just as, on the purely secular plane, world unification cannot be long delayed, so on the religious plane, the present melting pot of religion must, in the long run, simmer down into a coherent whole, and just as we cannot see how the antagonisms of personal, national, and ideological wills can be vanquished by any purely human agency, so we cannot see how first a divided Christianity can be united, nor how, beyond Christendom, the non-Christian religions can either absorb or be absorbed into Christianity. This, however, is to reckon without a power that is greater than man, greater than nations, and greater than individual religions.[14]

Church Universality and Man's Desire
for Convergence

This section shows the influence of Teilhard on Zaehner. Books such as Matter and Spirit, Concordant Discord, and Evolution in Religion devote lengthy sections to Teilhard's insights. In particular, Vedanta spirituality and Marxism are studied as alternatives to Christianity as a means of providing an integrating center which man seeks. Both Vedanta and Marxism lack a center with truly universal appeal. But for Teilhard and Zaehner the Church, in theory at least, is universal enough, a true center, to allow man to fully achieve himself in communion with his fellow man.

---

logical conclusion, for once the apostolic authority of the Catholic Church had been rejected, then there was no legitimate authority that could take its place." Zaehner, Drugs, Mysticism, and Make-Believe, p. 199.

[14]Zaehner, Matter and Spirit, p. 18.

Modern industrial civilization, by separating
man from his roots in nature, has also deprived him
of his traditional religious roots. Christianity is
perhaps fortunate in that it was the first of the
great religions to face up to the enormous social
changes that industrialization brought in its wake;
it has had nearly two hundred years in which to
adapt itself to the scientific age. It has had
time to prepare its defense against the forces of
scientific age. It has had time to prepare its
defense against the forces of scientific materialism
and meet the challenge that science seemed to present to religious belief. Technology then, is
creating conditions which make individual effort
futile and closest cooperation inevitable: it
forces unity upon us on the material plane. It is
not only the duty of the Christian Church to expand
into that universality she has always claimed is
here. It is a function thrust on her by history and
evolution itself.[15]

All the religions will be faced with the twin
challenges of materialistic secularism and Marxian
Communism with which Christianity alone is fully
familiar. How far the purely immanentist religions
which originate in India will be able to meet this
challenge remains to be seen, for there is so much
in dialectical materialism that is akin to the dialectical thought of the Hindus and Buddhists that
their wholesale conversion to this new religion
which puts Nature in the place of God cannot be al-
together ruled out. Dialectical materialism's
irresistibility would be its success in re-creating
ancient doctrines in a modern "scientific" form.
Hence the importance of monotheistic religions which
affirm the reality and sovereignty of God over
against Nature and all the created order. Of these
Jewry and Christianity have been tested by the
technological age. For Islam the time of testing
is yet to come.[16]

Modern science then, challenges all religions. Religions respond to the encounter in various
ways. Zaehner feels that with the possible

---

[15]Ibid., p. 206.

[16]Zaehner, The Concise Encyclopedia of
Living Faiths, p. 417.

exception of Christianity, the religions of the
world are actually ill-equipped for the encounter.

> . . . the Eastern religions can scarcely stand
> up to the assault of western science. Despite
> the sublimity of the concepts, no purely mytho-
> logical deity, no Krishna or Bodhisattva, can
> for long hold the allegiance of modern man, nor
> can the mysticism of escape any longer satisfy,
> for it concerns the individual alone, and man-
> kind is tiring of individuality and demands a
> religion that provides for the salvation and
> sanctification of the whole human race. Thus,
> while it is possible that the Neo-Vedanta and
> Zen Buddhism may satisfy some individuals for a
> short time, they plainly can never be inte-
> grated into modern society. Neither Confucian-
> ism nor Taoism was able to stand up to the
> impact of a militant Marxism. For Islam . . .
> all attempts to bring it into harmony with the
> modern age have so far failed.[17]

Zaehner once again turns to Teilhard who in
this case criticizes Vedanta and Marxism for their
deficiency in finding a true universal center.
Teilhard saw that we live in time, in evolutionary
time, and we are not static entities but parts of a
process. We proceed and ascend from the pure multiplicity of primal matter towards the pinnacle of
spirit. In Teilhard's words this is the Christ-
Omega, the point into which the whole universe must
converge. Only there can there be a universal

---

[17]Zaehner, Matter and Spirit, p. 185. This
is an attitude repeated in several of Zaehner's
writings. It is present as far back as 1956: "The
Religious Instinct," p. 83. He also writes: "For
the other religions the testing time has come only
now. The Asiatic countries have at last realized
that, if they wish to speak to the West on equal
terms, they can only do so if they are materially,
as well equipped as they. This means industrialization and all its challenges. This is the purely
outward aspect of Asia's awakening. On the religious
side there is a new self confidence among an elite
and an assertion of the values of Asian religion."
Zaehner, Concise Encyclopedia of Living Faiths,
p. 403.

mystical life in which death will be conquered and "God will be all in all" (1 Cor. 15:28).[18] While admitting that Vedanta, by which he means all Hindu and Buddhist mysticism, is, together with Marxism, the only valid alternative to a revitalized and fully evolutionary Christianity, he sees in it only a reversion to a more primitive state of mind that may have existed before self-consciousness was born. It is not a broadening of consciousness directed towards a universal center which for Teilhard is the cosmic Christ. It is rather a merging and dissipation of the infant ego into the unconscious matter from which it had so laboriously evolved. It is essentially retrograde and the enemy of all progress.[19]

Teilhard chooses Christianity as the viable alternative for mankind for it strikes the necessary balance between what he considers the extremes of the other two, i.e., excessive reliance on matter or an overly restrictive interiority that sees the world's evolution as illusion. Buddhism, for Teilhard, represents the same kind of spirituality as Sankara's Vedanta; it is not primarily interested in the world (while for Aurobindo its mysticism was too negative and dualist in its Therevada form).[20]

Aurobindo could find no center or principle of unity within Hinduism since, socially, Hinduism has hitherto been based on caste and even today the

---

[18]Zaehner, _Evolution in Religion_, p. 45.

[19]Ibid., p. 18. Zaehner agrees that this is in essence the mysticism of the earlier Upanishads. But he also criticizes Teilhard as being wrong in writing off eastern mysticism as "dated." Teilhard criticized only one tendency in eastern mysticism, the tendency to renounce the world rather than to merge into it so as the better to dominate it. Although Teilhard admired the passion for unity in eastern religions he seems to have reacted against Sankara's illusionism and the world denying austerity of Theravada Buddhism. But this is less than half of the Indian religion and was criticized by Aurobindo also. Zaehner, _Evolution in Religion_, p. 23.

[20]Zaehner, _Evolution in Religion_, p. 16.

Sankaracarya of Puri can defend not only the caste system but also untouchability. It is yet too early to know if Aurobindo himself can suffice as a principle of unity.[21]

Christianity, on the other hand, is both "this worldly" and "other worldly." It is equipped to face the technological world, says Zaehner, because of its balanced view on matter-spirit, nature-grace. In the Incarnation these orders combine to build up the mystical body of the risen Christ.

For all the good that Marxism can provide, it too lacks a rational vision capable of cementing together not only men's bodies in an ordered society, but also men's minds and souls in a common sense of purpose, a common drive toward human fulfillment. This alone the Church can provide, for it is built upon the Son of God, who as the "All Man," is the magnet of human unity, upon which all striving toward unification must ultimately converge. Marxism cannot supply the magnet owing to its defective view of matter. Teilhard has shown us on the other hand, how God works through matter itself for our own sanctification.[22] The Marxist view of matter is not rejected totally. It is seen as deficient but yet containing a valuable orientation. "The mysticism of Teilhard is grounded in matter but refuses the temptation to return to the inert state of primal matter which seems to be characteristic of Taoism: it is the aspiration of matter towards spirit, of multiplicity towards unity--directed not to the past but in Messianic hope to the future--a Marxist mysticism for which perhaps the world may be becoming ripe."[23]

Teilhard can be called a Marxist in the

---

[21]Ibid., p. 13. Despite his distaste for organized religion Aurobindo realized that the Catholic principle within Christianity was the nearest approximation in the history of the religions to his own vision of a humanity redeemed and divinized. He thought that the Reformation had thwarted a drive towards unity. Ibid., p. 25.

[22]Zaehner, Matter and Spirit, p. 208.

[23]Zaehner, Concordant Discord, p. 422.

sense that he accepted the socialization that Engels intended, i.e., an existence guaranteeing, by means of social production, material sufficiency as well as the exercise of physical and spiritual faculties. But as a Christian Teilhard had to go further: he had to reinfuse the spirit into a spiritless situation, and find a new heart for a heartless world. For Teilhard the way to go further was to accept the Incarnation of Christ because through it the sanctification of matter begins. Sanctification, like creation, means to unite, to draw all that is disparate into a coherent whole, and this is the force which continues to operate in evolutionary, human history. One may call it the vital life-spirit with Marx. Teilhard would call it the Holy Spirit and would do so with a purpose. For even if the Marxist vision sees the flux of matter directed, in Teilhard's words, "towards some kind of <u>collective</u> reflection and sympathy in which everyone can share by participation . . . and in which each human being would find his intellectual and affective fulfillment by forming one body with the whole," still it lacks two things. It lacks a true center of convergence which will make physical death irrelevant, and it turns its back on love: it lacks the Word made flesh and rejects the Holy Spirit.[24]

The lack of a center, says Zaehner, was the one missing element in the Zoroastrian vision of the solidarity of mankind as it is lacking in the Marxist vision of the future classless state. Without a center the members lack a source of strength or a means of co-ordinating their activities.

Both edifices lack a cornerstone made of living rock, and so the one collapsed as the other must in its turn collapse unless and until it grafts itself on to the temple that has for two thousand years been growing up upon the rock of Peter and beyond Peter, Christ . . . for no religion has eternal life unless it is anchored to a foundation that is itself eternal. How much less, then, can Marxism last, moored as it is in no visible or invisible center, yet knowing in its bones that without such a center it must

---

[24]Ibid., p. 423.

73

disintegrate.[25]

On the other hand Christ came as "the bond
of union that was to draw all men together into his
own body which is the church. His mission was not
only to reunite man with God, but to heal the
lesion between soul and body in individual men, and
to build them into the integrated whole which is the
church.[26]

Zaehner is saying, then, that at this time
in history the Christian church alone is a true
center of convergence. Mankind looks for a "locus"
which responds to his desire for universality in
which man can fully achieve himself in communion with
his fellow man. Finding Vedanta and Marxism deficient for this task, Zaehner presents the ideal of
the Christian Church as the organism which can unite
man into one body. This is an ideal and as we shall
see later perhaps too far removed from practical
fulfillment to be convincing or useful.

The Church as Fulfillment of Man's Religious Aspirations

The second part of chapter two presented
Christ as the fulfillment of man's religious aspirations. Since Zaehner sees the church as an extension of Christ in time and history, it is not
surprising that he presents the church too as a
fulfillment of man's religious aspirations. He does
this by showing that the church strikes a balance
between the extremes of other religions, or else
combines into harmony the various elements necessary

---

[25]Zaehner, <u>Matter and Spirit</u>, pp. 194-95.

[26]Ibid., p. 194. He also notes: "Man's
tragedy since Adam fell is that he is alone: the
existential tragedy is that not only is he alone,
but that he knows he is alone. Classical Buddhism
tells us how to be alone, but it does not tell us
how to 'bring forth much fruit.' Marxism tells us
how to bring forth much fruit, but it does not tell
us how to put back a heart into a heartless world."
Zaehner, <u>Matter and Spirit</u>, p. 183.

to produce religious wholeness in man.

As we have already indicated several of
Zaehner's books have been largely inspired by the
writings of Teilhard de Chardin. It should not be
surprising then, to find the church described in
evolutionary terms. Thus, the ancient Christian
doctrine of the "mystical" body of Christ is seen
as a culminating point of the evolutionary process
itself. This vision of the church goes beyond personal salvation to an emphasis on human solidarity
and salvation. A narrow individualism cedes to a
collective civilization yet to be born.

Zaehner tries to show that from the beginning there has been, within religions, two tendencies in tension with each other--the one drawing the
individual ever deeper into himself, and the other
integrating him more closely with the religious
community. In Christian terminology this means the
tension between preoccupation with individual salvation and the building up of the body of Christ in
the Church. Teilhard has put the concept of the
growing into fullness of the mystical body of Christ
in his church into the forefront of his conception
of Christianity. His integral "catholic" vision saw
the communal role of man in which each depends on
all and all on each. His vision is the slow convergence of all man's religious thinking into the
Catholic Church which is now in the process of being
built up and which, under the "Convergent spirit"
that informs it, must ultimately reach its full ex-
pansion in that it will come to include all men.[27]

The Indians are "solitary," the Chinese "solidary." In the West the Catholic Church is or
should be both--making room both for the "to-
getherness" of our mechanized age and for the
solitude in which all of us would do well from
time to time to renew our spiritual life if we
have one. . . . This is a tension and at the
same time a reconciliation. . . . Perhaps as

[27]Zaehner, Matter and Spirit, pp. 18-19. It
should be remembered that broadly speaking there are
religions of solitude (India and Taoism) and religions of solidarity (Israel, Confucianism and later
Islam). Zaehner, Evolution in Religion, p. 96.

de Chardin said, the age of Religion as opposed to the age of religions is only just beginning, and that religion may yet be in Marx's words "the heart of a heartless world."[28]

Seen in this context the Catholic Church is the middle way between the quest for individual salvation so typical of India and the quest for the corporate harmony of a perfect society that was China's ideal; it is the middle way between the absolute transcendence of the Muslim God and the absolute immanence of the Hindu Absolute, for the transcendent and immanent meet absolutely only in one place, in the God-man, Jesus Christ.[29]

For Christians Jesus is God made man, and this makes it impossible to treat Christianity simply as a prophetic religion. From the very beginning a mystical element is present, and it is this if anything, that entitles Christianity to speak of itself as unique. It cannot be broadly classified as either prophetic or mystical: it falls somewhere between the two.[30]

Actually, the fulfillment themes applied to Christ in chapter two apply in much the same way to the Church. This follows since the Church is seen as the body of Christ and the continuation of the Incarnation. Even when Zaehner contrasts individual and communal salvation he is working against a fulfillment theme background. The Church steers a middle course between these two extremes and thus blends both poles into a unity. Or, from another viewpoint, this _via media_ seems to "offer something

---

[28]Zaehner, _Concordant Discord_, p. 213. Zaehner notes that the Gita is an exception to "solitary" mysticism in India. The Gita asks for the integration of oneself around one's own immortal core thereby to become free to see oneself in all things and all things in oneself. Having seen this you will see all things in God and God as the ground of all things. Cf. _Concordant Discord_, p. 213.

[29]Zaehner, _Christianity and Other Religions_, p. 148.

[30]Zaehner, _Concordant Discord_, p. 24.

for everyone." No matter what man's religious aspirations are he can find a tradition within the Church which will respond to that aspiration. The same kind of reasoning is applied to the contrast between immanent, mystical religions and transcendent, prophetic religions. Here too the church appears as a _via media_.

This, of course, gives the impression that this balance has been and is presently maintained. The practical situation is another question. It is easy to accept that the Catholic Church is de jure the one human organization that can claim the allegiance of all mankind because in the person of Jesus and the church he founded are fulfilled both the inspired insights of the Hindus and Mahayana Buddhists which point to the potential deification of all human beings in the all-embracing love of the one God, and the social ideal of the Neo-Confucianists which envisaged a harmonious society of perfected beings under the sway of the one Supreme Ultimate. But sin in the church prevents the church from being the Catholic Church de facto, i.e., the community for which Christ gave his life that all men might be made whole and in which they might be integrated. It is the church as it does not exist now but will be at the end of time.[31]

In order to be more like the Church de facto in our present time, Zaehner acknowledges the Church's need to turn to the mystical traditions of the East. This the church should do to rediscover her own mystical tradition and redress the balance between mystical and prophetic tradition within Christianity.

We cannot afford to neglect the witness of the Eastern religions, for they emphasize, perhaps too much, an aspect of Catholicism that has been allowed to fade ever since the reformation wrested our gaze from the God who dwells within us. . . . In so far as we have allowed ourselves to be knocked off that perfect yet precarious balance between the transcendent Lord and Judge and the indwelling Christ we renew in ourselves each time we receive Holy Communion a balance

---

[31]Zaehner, Christianity and Other Religions, p. 147.

which it is the Church's mission to preserve--
to that extent we have distorted Catholic truth.[32]

Actually, what Zaehner does is repeat, on a
different level, the arguments for Christ as the
fulfillment of man's religious aspirations which were
treated in chapter two. Since the church is the
continuation of Christ in time the arguments concerning Christ are applied in a parallel way to the
church. The general argument from "fulfillment" has
both strength and weakness as we shall see in chapter five. These qualities apply equally well to
Christ as to the Church.

The Eucharist as a Symbol of Unity

Zaehner's understanding of the Eucharist is
treated in this chapter because the Eucharist is a
symbol of Christ and his church. The Eucharist,
though, is not only a special presence of the risen
Christ, nor only the nourishment of the body of
Christ, the church. It is also the symbol and cul-
mination of all that the church is supposed to be
especially in her unity.

By his resurrection Christ sanctifies our
flesh and promises that we too will be resurrected
in a "spiritual body." After the resurrection, however, Christ ceases to be simply a man. He is the
new All-man who is present all over the earth in
the sacrament of bread and wine and in the living
organism of the church. Sacrament and church represent the Catholic unity of the body of Christ.[33]

The unity symbolized by the Eucharist repeats
in its own way the unity wrought by Christ and by
the Church. Just as Christ and Church witness to
the unity of matter and spirit, so too the Eucharist
makes the same witness. Just as Christ and church
unite individual and communal salvation, so too the
Eucharist is a symbol of individual and communal
salvation.

---

[32]Ibid., p. 130.

[33]Zaehner, Evolution in Religion, p. 110.

Zaehner sees the Eucharist as a symbol of
the union of matter and spirit because in institu-
ting the sacrament of bread and wine Christ conse-
crates and converts into himself the whole of the
material universe that converges upon man, who is
the rational apex of evolution. Christ identifies
our daily food and drink, the bread and wine of the
sacrament, with his own body and blood. If we are
members of the body of Christ we live by the life of
that body, it is the Spirit who gives life, the
same Spirit who from the beginning quickened matter.[34]

It is the Spirit who transforms matter (bread
and wine) into spiritual food which in turn transforms our bodies more and more into Spirit. Thus
because one has this enduring symbol of transformed
matter Zaehner says that: the Eucharist forever
heals the breach between matter, and spirit and the
breach between God and man. It is a symbol of what
is to transpire in creation and in every person.
"Few of us are mystics, and it is because the Catholic Church brings the surety of mystical union with
the Incarnate God to ordinary man in the Blessed
Sacrament that even ordinary men are enabled to
taste, however faintly, the things God has prepared
for those who love him."[35] "Before he died, Christ
instituted the sacrament of unity, the material
sacrament of his own body and blood mysteriously
present in the consecrated bread and wine, the
sacramental centre and focus of unity, the food
that transforms our carnal body into a spiritual
body so that all might grow together into his mystical body which is the church."[36]

---

[34]Zaehner, Matter and Spirit, p. 201.

[35]Zaehner, Christianity and Other Religions,
p. 148.

[36]Zaehner, Evolution in Religion, p. 75.
Zaehner emphasizes that Christianity is the reli-
gion of the Word made flesh, and not only Jesus of
2,000 years ago but present now in the Eucharist.
This is the essential difference between Christians
and Muslims: for the Muslims the Word is made Book.
There is also a gulf, he says, between biblical
Protestantism and sacramental Catholicism. Zaehner,
Concordant Discord, p. 383.

As was mentioned the Eucharist is also a
symbol of individual and communal salvation. As a
symbol of individual salvation the Eucharist is a
bond of unity, but it is also the re-enactment of
the self-sacrifice of the God-man on the cross.
To partake of the Eucharist means to strive for the
attitude of selflessness which kills self-love, to
die to oneself as completely as did Jesus on the
cross. This attitude is the condition for all men
to arrive at union with God or with fellow-man,
regardless of his religious faith. This is the condition of "resurrection," of the final spiritualization of the individual monad, which is achieved by
following Christ's example. This death to the individual is continually signified by the Eucharist.

The Eucharist is also a symbol of man's collective salvation. It symbolizes and continues to
be the presence of Christ whose self-sacrifice on
the cross, in the Christian view, redeemed all men.
Out of the self-sacrifice grew the solidarity of
Pentecost which was a reversal of the disruption
symbolized by the tower of Babel. Since the time of
Pentecost it has been in principle, at least, the
role of the Catholic Church to manifest the solidarity and unity which Christ inaugurated. The
Church "realized that the principle of unity lay
not so much in the Pope, as in the Mass, the never-
ending repetition in time of the self-sacrifice of
the cross out of which grew the solidarity of the
first Pentecost."[37]

According to de Chardin, redemption will come
for it is inbuilt in the process of evolution itself.
Individual redemption finds its fulfillment in a
collective apotheosis where individuals are centered
on one common ultimate center in whom they can reach
their own entire fulfillment, by uniting. In
Zaehner's view this "ultimate center" is already
here. It is in the sacrament of bread and wine, the
body and blood of the Man-God Jesus, killed and ne-
gated as a single man on the cross, and resurrected
as our universal food, that the Church realizes herself as the Soul of the World. United with Jesus,
the Spirit advances to what Teilhard calls Omega,
the final point of union, bringing with him all

---

[37]Zaehner, Dialectical Christianity and
Christian Materialism, p. 94.

that can be saved, all that wants to be saved.[38]

Zaehner's Theoretical-Practical
Criticism of the Church

Zaehner views the Church as a focal point of unity for mankind. This follows from the close connection which he sees between Christ and the Church. But his evaluation of the Church is tempered by the real situation in which he sees it, i.e., a church subject to sin; a church which works as counter-sign as well as a sign of Christ. "It has often been said that the strongest argument against the Christian religion is the Christians themselves. This is true."[39]

Christianity is supposed to be a religion of love. This was never true except at the very beginning: after the Reformation neither side bothered to conceal its ferocious hatred of the other. The justification of persecution by the great Augustine and the fratricidal wars of the Reformation period gave the lie to the Christian claim that the Christian religion was based on love . . . the reign of charity is only a far-off dream.[40]

To the shame of the church much of its history has been marred by forgetfulness of its spiritual task. Since the time of Constantine, says

---

[38]Ibid., pp. 95-96.

[39]Zaehner, Concordant Discord, p. 366. "It is obvious that the Catholic Church is the natural rallying-point of all believers in God as opposed to those who equate him with nature. Yet, though this is true, and though the Catholic Church is incomparably the most cohesive, the most vital and the most universal religious organization in the world, she nevertheless has a capacity of attracting to herself repugnance and hatred." Zaehner, "The Religious Instinct," p. 84.

[40]Zaehner, Concordant Discord, p. 377.

81

Zaehner, the church has succumbed to temptation.
The temptations are various and poorly resisted:
over-involvement in money, power and politics. "The
Bride of Christ had become the Whore of Babylon."[41]
The very community that had been promised persecution by its founder turned to persecution itself. In
the name of universality and unity, intolerance and
Inquisition has tried to accomplish that which
only the Spirit of God can produce. This sad side
of the Church's history is too well known and
wearisome to recount. But Zaehner mentions it
because the attitude remains, to some degree, with
the church.

Fully conscious of the church's failings,
Zaehner uses the image of the Church as spouse of
Christ. At the same time his chapter on the church
in the Gifford Lectures was entitled: "Hosea's
Wife"; the church at once spouse and whore. Elsewhere he notes: "'Christ's way' is the highway of
the church--both the Church as 'It,' the impersonal
'sacrament machine' which thrives on the law and
theology and is run for the most part by mediocre
scribes, and the church as 'She,' spouse and whore,
the church of sinners even more than the church of
saints, sinning again, but always rising again,
reaching out in hope to the 'summit of her joy.'"[42]

The Church is still wracked and riddled with
human sin. It has a history of bloodshed, persecution and bigotry behind it.

We must never forget the sufferings that the
Church has from time to time inflicted on sincere men who could not see in her the true Church
of Christ because she herself had marred the
image; and, just as Gandhi saw in untouchability
an "ineffaceable blot" and a "curse" that had
fallen on Hinduism, so must we see that persecution, forced conversions, the burning of here-
tics, and all the other crimes that have been
perpetrated in the name of Christ are an "ineffaceable blot" and a "curse" for which penance
is still due. In the scale of time as evolution

---

[41]Ibid., p. 375.

[42]Zaehner, Drugs, Mysticism, and Make-Believe,
p. 210.

sees it, however, two thousand years is but a day, and we can only hope that the Church, to which all the other religions, in the course of their evolution, draw ever nearer in spirit and in doctrine, will one day so have purified herself that she will be able to show forth Jesus Christ not only as the true Messiah, but also as the true Krishna, and the true Bodhisattva who takes upon himself the burden of saving all sentient beings until the end of time.[43]

The foibles of the church have always been present. It will continue to be that way. Zaehner's basis for saying that is that Pentecost was the embryonic promise, not the adult fulfillment of the communion of Saints. The church has the guarantee but it has not yet the fulfillment, it is subject always and inexorably to sin because a collective egoism is put in the place of the free working of the Holy Spirit.[44]

Elsewhere Zaehner characterizes this guarantee in terms of potency and act, i.e., the church as it is now and as it can and ought to be. In regard to the recent renewal within the Roman Church he writes: "The Roman Church . . . transformed itself into something that was at least recognizable as an authentic member of the Church of Christ. The Roman church was seen to be not the Catholic Church indeed, since so many sincere Christians remained outside of it, but to be once again the Catholic Church in potency, for it would be foolish to suppose that there ever will be a Catholic Church in act until the end of time, if then."[45]

The growth of the church must be seen in evolutionary terms as Chardin says so often. And if it is true, as Psalm 65 states: "that a thousand years are as one day in the sight of God" then the church is only two days old, thus indicating that it is too soon to see the church as a focus of unity

---

[43]Zaehner, Christianity and Other Religions, p. 147.

[44]Zaehner, Evolution in Religion, p. 79.

[45]Zaehner, Concordant Discord, p. 13.

83

for mankind. "It may be millions of years before the corporate ideal of the church as the body of Christ ever begins to look like reality, but the Holy Spirit has all eternity in which to work."[46]

Indeed, says Zaehner, such a transformation would take a real miracle. With such a miracle the church will grow inwardly into a super consciousness manifesting itself in spontaneous love and joy leading to individual and corporate freedom.

> . . . having realized the kingdom of God within herself she may succeed in embracing the whole of humanity within the finally realized city of God on earth. The Catholic Church de jure might then become the Catholic Church de facto, and who knows, perhaps before the demise of this planet, having perfected herself on earth, she may be able to spread the gospel of sac-cid-ananda, of Being, Super-Consciousness, and spontaneous Joy, the Catholic gospel of unity in Trinity through the power of the Holy Spirit, throughout the entire universe.[47]

The Christian Church sees itself as a single organism in which the individual has his part to play and his individual soul to save. But this is secondary in the Church's mission which is to build the whole human race into the mystical body of Christ. Since the Reformation, Christians have been so divided that the ideal of integrating man within himself through Christ, of integrating him into the "body of Christ" which is the church, and of expanding that body, so that it will embrace all mankind, has often been allowed to slip into the background.[48]

---

[46]Zaehner, Evolution in Religion, p. 113.

[47]Ibid., p. 85 and also Christianity and Other Religions, pp. 146-47.

[48]Zaehner also writes: "Christ's indictment of the scribes and Pharisees is not simply an indictment of the religious establishment of his time: it is a permanent indictment of all religious establishments as such. It is an indictment not only of the Catholic hierarchy but much more of organized Protestantism which has always seemed to me to be the religion of the scribes par excellence." Zaehner,

Nevertheless, in the face of these obstacles, Zaehner values allegiance to the Church. He seems to equate his sentiments with those of Teilhard in saying:

Yet despite occasional bitterness it never seriously occurred to him (Teilhard) to leave the Society of Jesus, let alone the Roman Church, for despite all its defects it was for him the only possible center of unity in the frame of which the collective salvation of mankind could one day be realized. Despite its pettyfogging legalism and a sacramental system that has so often degenerated into an almost mechanical device by which salvation might be obtained, the Roman Church with the Supreme Pontiff as Vicar of Christ at its head was still the only possible focus of unity which acting as the axis of evolution itself, could mould mankind together into a unified and forward-thrusting collectivity destined ultimately to converge upon God as its true and predestined Centre.[49]

Zaehner, then, works between a practical image of the church riddled by imperfection and an ideal image of what the church ought to be or will be in the future. The former often looks discouraging and seems to offer little hope of being in fact the focal point of man's unification. Yet, Zaehner clings to the ideal, holding it out as what at least ought to be.

The Christian Church represents only a fraction of mankind, but ideally the body of Christ should encompass the whole human race—how and in what form—we have not the slightest idea. . . . We can only look forward in faith to the day when all men will be "as living stone, built up, a spiritual house . . . acceptable to God by Christ Jesus" (1 Peter 2:5). And it will be not only our house but the house of all those who

---

Concordant Discord, p. 382.

[49]Zaehner, Evolution in Religion, p. 9.

from all the religions of the world may one day
see fit to pour their spiritual treasures into
it.[50]

---

[50]Zaehner, _Christianity and Other Religions_,
p. 148.

CHAPTER IV

ZAEHNER'S UNDERSTANDING OF MYSTICISM AS

A POINT OF DIALOGUE AND UNITY

BETWEEN RELIGIONS

This chapter does not attempt to evaluate all that Zaehner has proposed in his writings concerning mysticism. Rather, it looks at his appreciation of mysticism insofar as mysticism influences the dialogue between major world religions.

A) First of all, Zaehner stresses that there are varieties of mystical experiences. Another way of saying this is to say that not all mystical experiences are the same. To say that all mystical experiences are the same is, in Zaehner's view, contrary to available evidence, as well as a source of confusion in inter-religious dialogue. Religious unity is actually hindered when based on such a false premise.

B) Secondly, Zaehner divides the various mystical experiences into three general categories: nature mysticism, monistic mysticism, and theistic mysticism. It is the last two of these that Zaehner compares and distinguishes. They have different dogmatic foundations especially in relation to God. There can be no true dialogue without recognition of these differences. That it is actually impossible to hold monistic and theistic opinions as both being absolutely true at one and the same time, seems obvious.[1]

C) Thirdly, Zaehner argues that mysticism should find its perfection in theistic mysticism. The evidence for this, in Zaehner's view, is that one sees even in monistic traditions a movement towards

---

[1] Zaehner, _Mysticism Sacred and Profane_, p. xv.

87

theistic mysticism's goal of loving union with God. The mystic should be led beyond the realization of the "self" onward to God. This realization has been especially taught by Christ whose life and teaching bring a perfection to mysticism. This, once again, is a return to the fulfillment in Christ model.

The Plurality of Mystical Experiences

Zaehner has written quite extensively on the subject of mysticism. This is only natural since so many of the religions he has studied have a strong mystical bent. Indian religion in particular is for him mystical through and through. It is inevitable that his study of comparative religion involves his study of mysticism. Amid so many other discordant features between religions mysticism may be the most concordant feature at hand. With specific reference to inter-religious dialogue Zaehner notes: "The mystical prayer of the early church has much in common with the mystical insights of the Hindus, and most educated Hindus would agree that any approach to unity between great religions must be conducted on a mystical or contemplative plane."[2] As we shall see, though, there are dogmatic foundations behind mystical traditions. These contain elements of disunity as well as unity.

Zaehner agrees that there are many similarities among the various mystical traditions. To some

[2] Zaehner, Concordant Discord, p. 21. Zaehner disagrees with those who do not see the value of mysticism within the Christian tradition. He writes: "Mysticism, however, pace Dr. Kraemer, is part and parcel of the Christian tradition—of the Christian faith, and not merely of what he likes to call historical Christianity; and it is its mystical element that allows Christianity to be a 'light to lighten the Gentiles' and the fulfillment of their hopes. Here, and nowhere else, can it enter into a dialogue with Indian religion in terms that the latter can understand." Zaehner, At Sundry Times, p. 173.

extent mysticism cuts across religious lines.[3] But this is far different from saying that all mystical experiences are the same. In his judgment those who propose religious unity based totally upon mystical unity are in error. The following is an example with which Zaehner disagrees: "The only real heresy is to maintain that one religion only is in exclusive possession of the truth. All are rather facets of the same truth, this truth being presented in a different manner at different times in accordance with the spiritual development of the society to which it is directed. The truth itself is that experienced by the mystics whose unity of thought and language is said to speak for itself."[4]

Zaehner will assert that such a statement often cannot even be maintained within one and the same religious tradition, not to mention other traditions. So, he writes: "If in distinguishing between different types of mystical experience I have been forced to disagree with the conclusions of eminent writers, it is only because the over-simplification of the very complex problem of praeternatural and mystical experience seems to me to destroy, rather than to broaden, the basis of religion."[5]

Zaehner sets out to prove that mysticism is not a uniform phenomenon. In his opinion it is wrong to assume that mysticism is one and the same in all mystics as though there were not significant differences. Actually, in comparing various mystical traditions one sees at times similar phenomena, as well as distinctive characteristics. What goes by the name of mysticism, so far from being an identical expression of the selfsame Universal Spirit, falls into distinct categories. This is true at

---

[3]For Zaehner mysticism is a study of the praeternatural experiences in which sense perception and discursive thought are transcended in an immediate apperception of a unity or union which is apprehended as lying beyond and transcending the multiplicity of the world as we know it.

[4]Zaehner, Mysticism Sacred and Profane, p. 27.

[5]Ibid., p. v.

times even within one particular religious tradition.

The immediate occasion of Zaehner's first book on Mysticism was the publication of A. Huxley's The Doors of Perception. Huxley had in effect lumped together all mystical experiences. This was, for Zaehner, fraught with danger. It carelessly overlooked distinctive mystical attitudes which ultimately had serious religious consequences. Hence Zaehner wrote Mysticism Sacred and Profane whose main themes have been repeated in later books and articles.

Zaehner confesses that at age twenty he experienced what is called "a natural mystical experience." This experience is very similar to the one that Mr. Aldous Huxley described in his book The Doors of Perception which Huxley says was an experience of the beatific vision. In response to this claim Zaehner asserts that the beatific vision, the direct experience of God in his holiness, has no connection with the natural mystical experience. The experience in itself is one thing, but it is quite distinct from the transports of the Christian and Muslim saints as well as from the "self-realization" and "self-isolation" of the Hindus. Huxley seemed to assume that all praeternatural experiences described by the all-embracing term "mysticism" must be the same in essence, no matter if they resulted from asceticism, Yoga or drugs. But, says Zaehner, mescalin is also clinically used to produce states akin to schizophrenia and mania. In fact the experience of manic-depressives shows a marked resemblance to Huxley's experience and to some more conventional mystics.

> It must therefore follow, if we accept the fatal "platitude" (mysticism is essentially one and the same), that not only can mystical experiences be obtained artifically through drugs, but is also naturally present in the manic. It must then follow that the vision of God of the mystical saint is "one and the same" as the hallucination of the lunatic. There would appear to be no way out unless the original "platitudinous" premiss is unsound.[6]

---

[6]Ibid., p. xi. Two psychiatrists have taken exception to what they consider Zaehner's contemptuous reference to lunatics. They argue against

Zaehner also comments on the religious and moral consequences of such a position:

If we have been right in identifying the natural mystical experience which Huxley sampled under the influence of mescalin and which comes to others unexpectedly and quite unsummoned, with what is technically called mania, and if both are to be explained as a direct experience of what, for lack of a more precise word, we still must call the collective unconscious, then it must follow that the next stage, the integration of the unconscious and the conscious mind in the "self," must be a more advanced stage. Thus, if as Huxley once maintained, he could understand precisely what is meant by the beatific vision when still under the influence of mescalin, it would seem to follow assuming that by that statement that he actually meant that he was really enjoying that vision—that the beatific vision is a state that can be transcended. If this is really so, then it can be induced by drugs, and that since the vision makes nonsense of common morality, let alone the virtues of humility and charity, then the picture of God which we derive from Jesus of

Zaehner what they consider an alternative hypothesis. They hold as plausible that some mystical saints and some lunatics are undergoing essentially the same class of experience, although with different particular details, in very different personal and cultural settings. The differences between mysticism and lunacy can be attributed to the details and settings and not, as Zaehner claims, to an experience of different entities—a real God on one hand and unreal lunacy or counterfeits on the other. They go further, maintaining that the criteria that Zaehner gives for distinguishing between sacred and profane mysticism do not bear criticism. R. Osmond and J. Smythies, "The Significance of Psychotic Experience: A Reply to Prof. Zaehner," The Hibbert Journal 57 (April 1959):241. Concerning mysticism and lunacy or schizophrenia cf. John White, ed., The Highest States of Consciousness (New York: Doubleday, 1972), esp. chs. 9, 10, 12, 13.

Nazareth must be false.[7]

The confusion that is popularly made between
nature mysticism and the mysticism of the
Christian saints can only discredit the latter.
By making the confusion one is forced into the
position that God is simply another term for
Nature; and it is an observable fact that in
Nature there is neither morality nor charity nor
even common decency. God then is reduced to
the sum total of natural impulses in which the
terms "good" and "evil" have no meaning. Such
a god is sub-human, a god unfit for rational
creatures.[8]

What will become more evident in what follows is that there are varieties of mystical experiences. There are different mystical traditions with
different dogmatic presuppositions leading to varying
religious conclusions and practices. It is therefore a mistake to lump together all mystical
experiences. That would only confuse the dialogue
between world religions.

Three Basic Categories of
Mystical Experiences

Since Zaehner claims that there are variations of mystical experience at this point we ask:

---

[7]Zaehner, Mysticism Sacred and Profane,
p. 124. Zaehner feels that not only do some erroneously equate different mystical traditions, but
also erroneously equate mystical experience with a
drug or psychedelic experience. He writes: "Just
as there are varieties of psychedelic experience
so there are varieties of mystical experience in
Hinduism, Islam, Christianity, and Buddhism. So to
say: 'It is not a matter of psychedelic experience
being similar to mystical experience: it is mystical
experience,' is misleading and provocative."
Zaehner, Drugs, Mysticism, and Make-Believe, p. 103.

[8]Zaehner, Mysticism Sacred and Profane,
p. 200.

"What are these different types?" We will summarize
three basic forms of mysticism which Zaehner distinguishes to show that there are various kinds of
mystical experience as well as to highlight their
basic differences. The differences give evidence
of varying religious attitudes which ultimately preclude a too-facile religious unity and harmony.

1) In nature mysticism the barrier between
the "self" and the "Not self," the experiencing subject and the objective world seem to vanish, and all
is seen as one and one as all. This mysticism can
be experienced by peoples of all religions or of no
religion at all. Individuality seems to dissolve
bringing joy and peace. One feels a strange identity with all that is because one sees and senses
the eternal in the temporal. It is the experience of
one as all and all as one. There is an experience of
oneness with nature and indeed of all things. For
this reason the terms "nature mystic" and "cosmic
consciousness" have been used to describe the experience. Since the experience need not relate to God
Zaehner dislikes calling it pantheistic. He prefers
the word "panenhenism," i.e., "all-in-one-ism." The
experience may occur in a moment, unsolicited, without religious connotations. Some men who have
experienced and described this mystical insight are
R. M. Bucke, W. Whitman, and as mentioned A. Huxley
whose experience was drug-induced.

Zaehner admits that nature mystics see the
harmony pervading all created things. It is much
akin to the Chinese experience of pushing back to a
harmony somehow sensed as a twilight age when men
lived in harmony with the world and divine law.
Nature mysticism is the experience of the oneness
and harmony of creation before it was spoilt by sin.
But the experiences of nature mysticism, despite the
joy and peace they bring, are nevertheless regres-
sions to a world of innocence that was shattered
when Adam fell. The experience of harmony may be
real, but the discord, misery and strife in which
we live are no less real.[9]

---

[9]Zaehner, Christianity and Other Religions,
pp. 132-35; Mysticism Sacred and Profane, chs. 3
and 4; Concordant Discord, ch. 3.

2) The second type is characterized as "solitary" or "monistic" mysticism. The mysticism of India, more strongly than any other tradition, has emphasized two levels of the person: a higher and a lower self. The latter is the selfish and rather superficial external self usually associated with the first person singular. The former is the hidden, spiritual, eternal self meant to be awakened by contemplation. In Zaehner's view it is this higher, transcendent self which is the object of the Hindu and Buddhist quest. It is the quest to reach one's "real self."

The habitat of the real self is beyond space and time in an eternal "now": it knows neither past nor future--it simply is. This sense of timelessness which is much less stressed in Catholic mysticism than it is in Hinduism and Buddhism, does not necessarily bring with it any awareness of God as a person distinct from oneself. It is, however, accompanied by a sense of immortality because what exists outside of time cannot die. It is usually accompanied by an experience of absolute oneness, which is felt to be an ultimate, beyond which, it seems, it is impossible to proceed. In this experience there is no knowledge of God as distinct from the eternal, real self. With no knowledge of God there is no love of Him. This is the mysticism of the "self" without conscious reference to God.

It is the experience of the oneness of the transcendent self, separate and isolated from the world of matter and mind as well as from all other "selves," even including God. This we meet within certain Hindu writings and also among certain Sufi mystics. It is probably what the Theravada Buddhists understand by Nirvana. It can be tasted by all men for this is the image of God in the human soul which at times, says Zaehner, he mistakes for the Godhead itself, as the non-dualist Vedanta did, and as Vivekananda has done in recent times.[10]

---

[10]Zaehner, Christianity and Other Religions, pp. 19-20 and 133; Concordant Discord, ch. 5. It should be noted that the system proposed by Shankara is known as Advaita or non-Dualist Vedanta because of his insistence that Brahman is the "ONE without a second." But also within the Vedanta tradition other interpretations of the Brahma sutras were

Actually in discussing monism, Zaehner concentrates on the non-dualist Vedanta school and the Samkhya Yoga school which we will discuss here briefly.

Hindu mysticism originates in the Upanishads where no clear distinction is drawn between the human soul which is regarded as being eternal by nature, and God. In the Vedanta self-realization is necessarily interpreted as meaning that the soul realizes itself as the Absolute. The same experience is interpreted by the Samkhya-Yoga as meaning no more than that the soul enjoys its own individual eternity.

In the Upanishads the Vedantin mystics understand Brahman as the source of all things and as including all things. It is greater than the universe yet the center of all hearts. For them Brahman is the universe, it is the soul. The soul realizes its complete identity with the absolute One.

On the other hand, in the Samkhya-Yoga system the final goal is the seeking of one's immortal soul in its nakedness and isolation. One does not seek union with God. Each soul is totally distinct from other souls and there can be no communion between them. One is to come to self-realization which is the isolation of the soul from all that is not itself.

It is a debatable point, and to some people highly objectionable, to include so great a writer and mystic as Sankara in the Samkhya-Yoga system. Zaehner feels that this is permissible because of Sankara's idea of mystical self-understanding. In Zaehner's view, by establishing complete identity between the human soul and the Absolute Sankara and his school do accept the Samkhya-Yoga view in practice. In fact Zaehner does see a similarity in practice between the Samkhya-Yoga school and the non-dualist Vedantins.[11] To be sure, there are

---

given in opposition to Snankara. The most important of these is the system of qualified non-Dualism of Ramanuja with its strongly theistic emphasis.

[11]Zaehner, Mysticism Sacred and Profane, pp. 203-204. John Chethimattam denies that Sankara's

differences of interpretation and theory between them. But ultimately they both are monistic in their goal. They both arrive at a "solitary" contemplation of the self which is not transcended. This is important for Zaehner for despite the varieties there is a basically recognizable category of monistic mysticism which will contrast sharply with his final category of theistic mysticism.

We should notice also that a mystic such as the Buddha rejects the world of matter. It is impermanent, subject to decay, and one cannot find salvation in it or through it. All attachment to the things of this world enslaves. There is one virtue necessary to salvation—detachment and withdrawal from both world and cosmos. Only so can you reach Nirvana, the ultimate peace beyond space and time.[12]

Even from these brief remarks one can see that the second type of mysticism is not identical with the panenhenic experience. Cosmic consciousness claims a oneness with the world and man. Monism avoids attachment to the world; it transcends both man and universe. Their messages are different. To say that the differences are merely a matter of interpretation is simply untrue.

Differences will also be noticed when we contrast monistic and theistic mysticism. Zaehner feels that both Christianity and Mahayana Buddhism disagree with the Samkhya and non-dualist Vedanta belief that once a man has realized his own timeless essence and entered Nirvana, he has reached a point beyond which it is impossible to proceed.[13]

---

system is a monism and explains that the negative "a" of "Advaita" only negates the world as a reality added to or in addition to the Absolute. J. Chethimattam, Consciousness and Reality (Bangalore: The Bangalore Press, 1967), p. 52.

[12]Zaehner, Concordant Discord, p. 60.

[13]Zaehner, Evolution in Religion, p. 107. According to Ninian Smart, Zaehner's classification of types of mysticism is unconvincing for Zaehner's evidence for his second type of mysticism (monism)

3) Zaehner also describes another type of
mysticism which is the normal type of Christian mystical experience in which the soul feels itself to
be united with God by love. The theological premiss
from which this experience starts is that the individual soul is created by God in His own image and
likeness from nothing, and that it has the capacity
of being united to God.

In Catholic mysticism,[14] the essential element is love. It is the direct experience here and

---

is drawn largely from an incorrect interpretation of
Indian religions, i.e., by lumping together three
very different views (Sankara, Samkhya-Yoga, and
Thoravada Buddhism) into the one category of monism.
Smart's view is that there is in essence one type of
dhyanic experience though it occurs in differing
contexts from Christianity to Theravada. N. Smart,
The Yogi and the Devotee (London: Allen and Unwin,
1968), pp. 71 and 73. In a personal interview at
Oxford, in May 1972 Zaehner claimed that Smart had
misunderstood him. Prof. Zaehner claimed that he
had maintained sufficient distinctions between
Samkhya-Yoga and Theravada Buddhism especially as
regards spirit and matter.

[14]Zaehner recognizes as a practical fact
that the present day church has to a large extent
lost its mystical bent. This he attributes to
staleness and lack of fervour. Nevertheless, owing
to the mystical tradition starting with St. Paul and
St. John which culminates in St. John of the Cross,
Zaehner considers mysticism as one of Catholicism's
essential elements. When Zaehner speaks of the mysticism of the Church he usually is speaking of
Catholicism. In Zaehner's view, Protestantism is
declared "anti-mystical," cf. At Sundry Times,
pp. 171-73; Christianity and Other Religions, p. 130;
Evolution in Religion, pp. 3, 24-25. Judaism is
also considered basically unmystical, cf. At Sundry
Times, p. 171. The same can be said for Islam with
the exception of Sufism, At Sundry Times, p. 116.
For a contrary opinion to those charges one can read
E. G. Parrinder, "Definitions of Mysticism," Hibbert Journal 70:3 (1972):312-15.

now of God's burning love for the soul and of the response of that soul. By the "soul" is meant, not the empirical "ego" but the true "transcendent self." It is the love of God for his own image in the human soul. It is the love of Person for person in which the two are ultimately to be made one. God takes the initiative and loves the soul. The soul is conscious that it is unworthy of this love and in need of the removal of sin and selfishness. The ultimate state of union is so intimate and humanity is so transformed that one speaks of the "deification" of the soul. This deification is a corollary of the Incarnation: God becomes man that man may become God. We have then, a personal encounter of the transcendent self with the living God and the realization of his infinite love. In this encounter the transcendent self itself realizes that the seeming infinity and timelessness it has learned to enjoy in itself is as nothing when confronted with the real infinity and majesty of God. It is a going beyond oneself to the love of God.

Mention should also be made of Muslim mysticism. It is Zaehner's contention that in Islam too there is a tendency towards theistic mysticism. Since Islam starts with a conception of God as wholly distinct from creation, as the completely other, it is difficult to find a basis for loving union between the utterly transcendent One and a mere creature.[15] Nevertheless, Sufism teaches that God can be experienced by those who wait upon his call with a loving heart. This will lead to union with God in which the soul still retains some trace of individuality.

---

[15]Zaehner also writes: "It can be maintained that the strictly monotheistic religions do not naturally lend themselves to mysticism; and there is much to be said for this view. The Torah and the Quran emphasize overwhelmingly the complete otherness of God. Christianity is the exception because it introduces into a monotheistic system an idea that is wholly foreign to it, namely, the Incarnation of God in Jesus Christ. Such an idea is repulsive to strict monotheism." R. C. Zaehner, Hindu and Muslim Mysticism (London: Athlone Press, 1960), p. 2.

It is true that there are also purely monistic ideas in Sufism which can be traced back to Abu
Yazid of Bistam. But it is Zaehner's contention
that he was directly influenced by the Vedanta.
Thus the purely monistic ideas in Abu Yazid or his
successors cannot be treated as independent evidence
for the ubiquity of the monist philosophy which is
sometimes held to underlie all manifestations of
mysticism. Still, the mysticism of Abu Yazid identified the soul with God, and this distortion
changed the course of Islamic mysticism.

Junayd of Baghdad, Ibn Tufayl, and Ghazali
opposed this view, declaring it to be an initial
isolation of the soul which had to be overcome by
God. If this were done then an I/thou relationship
could be established between the Soul and God.
Although there are various strands in the Sufi
tradition Zaehner views it as essentially a mysticism of love.

Whether or not Sufism can actually be reconciled with mainline Muslim teaching is another
question. "In Islam, we cannot help feeling that
Sufism is so radical a distortion of the orthodox
doctrine as to constitute almost a separate religion."[16] Zaehner is thus pointing out that even
in a monotheistic tradition that seemingly precludes
the creatures' attaining loving union with the
Creator, this mystical tendency towards love in
union emerged in it almost from the beginning.

We have, then, a third type of mysticism,
distinct from the other two. Whereas both theistic
and monist experiences are different from the pan-
en-henic experience, so do they differ from each
other.[17] For the theistic mystic something of the

---

[16]Zaehner, Hindu and Muslim Mysticism, p. 2.
A. C. Bouquet also writes: "It must be strictly
maintained that mysticism is not a natural growth
in Islam, but is a foreign element which has worked
its way into it, and is really inconsistent with the
original dogmas. It is perhaps a revolt of some
Moslem souls against the extremity of Islamic transcendence." A. C. Bouquet, Comparative Religion
(Baltimore: Penguin Books, 1969), p. 296.

[17]Zaehner, Mysticism Sacred and Profane,

soul must clearly remain if only to experience the
mystical experience. The individual is not anni-
hilated, although transformed and deified: it remains a distinct entity though permeated through and
through with the divine substance. For the monist
this is not so: the human soul is God or is totally
isolated in itself; there is no duality. This is not
to say that there are only differences between these
mystical experiences. But it is an affirmation that
there are in fact differences.[18]

The Argument for Theistic
Mystical Experience

It is especially the differences between
the second and third type of mysticism that influence
our study.[19] This is so because ultimately these
types of mysticism are based on diverging views of
God and the purpose of religious activity itself.
Unless these differences are acknowledged those in
the inter-religious dialogue will speak on different levels of understanding.

Here then are two distinct and mutually opposed
types of mysticism--the monistic and theistic.
This is not a question of Christianity and Islam

---

p. 29. Also Concordant Discord, chs. 6, 7, 8.

[18]Zaehner forestalls an objection to what he
has proposed. "I live now not with my own life but
with the life of Christ who lives in me" (Galatians
2:20). This is the aspect of Christ which the Neo-
Vedantins emphasize at the expense of all others--
the indwelling; but it is only one aspect. To live
with the life of Christ does not mean simply to sink
or rise into or rediscover a timeless joy within.
It means that, but also means to live as Christ lived,
selflessly in the service of other men. Zaehner,
Evolution in Religion, p. 97.

[19]Both Zaehner and N. Smart agree that "nature mysticism" should not really be classified as
mysticism. E. G. Parrinder disagrees in "Definitions
of Mysticism," p. 311.

versus Hinduism and Buddhism: it is an unbridgeable gulf between all those who see God as
incomparably greater than oneself, though He is,
at the same time, the root and ground of one's
being, and those who maintain that the soul and
God are one and the same and that all else is
pure illusion.[20]

For the monist, theistic mysticism is simply
devotion to a personal God carried to extremes. The
transports of the theistic mystic are regarded as an
early stage on the way to isolation, the stage of
bhakti which, for the monists, means paying homage
to a deity which one has imagined. The monist would
claim that to speak of unio mystica is merely to
misstate the case; reality is one, and if this is
really so, then to speak of union with God must be
meaningless.[21] On the other hand, the theist views
the monist's final stage as only the isolation of
the soul in natural rest. The monists' "liberation"
is simply the realization of one's soul in separation
from God, and, in the theist evaluation, this is only
a stage in the path of the beginner.[22]

Zaehner, however, does not leave his inquiry
on the level of difference in mysticism. He goes on

---

[20]Zaehner, _Mysticism Sacred and Profane_,
p. 204. Zaehner also says: "The fact that asceticism has been used in all religions as a means of
liberating spiritual energy does not, however, prove
that the goal of the religions on to which it is
grafted is necessarily the same. On the face of it,
it looks rather as if the same means are used in pur-
suit of different ends. And it is with ends that
dogma is concerned not means. . . . Religions are
based on dogmas. . . on certain fundamental assumptions. These form the ideological content of a given
religion." Zaehner, "Dogma," p. 14. It is Zaehner's
view that dogma, so far from being transcended by
ascetic practices, actually appears to condition the
state at which the ascetic aims.

[21]Zaehner, _Hindu and Muslim Mysticism_, p. 13.

[22]Zaehner, _Mysticism Sacred and Profane_,
pp. 204 and 206.

to make two arguments. 1) The Nirvana of the monistic mystics ought not to be the final goal of the mystic. The mystic ought to move beyond monism to loving union with God. Christianity is an ideal framework for this mysticism since it preserves Christ's teaching which brings a perfection to mysticism itself. 2) Even within Hinduism, Buddhism and Islam there is a strong element of theistic mysticism. This is, for Zaehner, evidence of an irresistable movement towards God as well as an indication of God's revelation of Himself in all religions. Let us examine this latter argument first.

There is only limited mention of love in the Upanishads, or the Samkhya-Yoga, or early Buddhism. Yet this is not surprising since man, in this view, makes the best of his nature on his own account. Even if God is helping man, the guidance will be done secretly and man will attribute the work to himself. The discovery of one's own transcendent self in the peace and joy of Nirvana was seen as man's goal. Since man seemingly could not go beyond Nirvana a loving union with God seemed superfluous and unwarranted.[23] Yet in Indian mysticism there is a slow advance towards the idea of a personal God who was distinct from the human soul. Even in its theistic development it did not at first move forward from a passive contemplation of the Lord in his solitary perfection to an active love of him.[24]

There are two passages in the Upanishads which speak of a state beyond dreamless sleep. These two passages between them represent two tendencies that were later to divide the allegiance of India's whole philosophical tradition: absolute monism on the one hand (Mandukya Upanishad) and qualified pluralism on the other (Chandogya Upanishad). Each gives a totally different view of what liberation means. Yet neither takes any cognizance of a personal God. But the extreme position of the Mandukya is far from typical of the Upanishads as a whole. Already in the Katha Upanishad the universal self is

---

[23]Zaehner, _Christianity and Other Religions_, p. 140.

[24]Zaehner, _Hindu and Muslim Mysticism_, p. 88.

identified with a creator God who chooses his elect.
In the Svetasvatara this idea is further developed,
and God the Creator and sustainer of all things,
asserts his supremacy over against the neuter absolute. It is clearly theistic.[25]

Another indication of loving union with God
is found in the Gita and also the saints of southern
India.[26] Herein was a recognition of the transcendent soul along with a recognition of its dependence
on a God who loved it. The detachment of the soul,
then, is only the prelude to an attachment, kindled
by love, to God who is the source of eternity--of
Brahman as much as he is the source of time.[27] The
core of the Gita is actually the theophany of chapter eleven, where God reveals Himself as Creator,
sustainer and destroyer of the universe. It shows a
marked progression from a monistic-pantheistic position to a theistic experience in which the soul
unites with the personal God Krishna in love.

Chapter five is also significant for here
Krishna indicates for the first time that liberation
from the bonds of matter, important as it may be, is
perhaps not in itself man's ultimate goal. In chapter six, Krishna shows that to experience Brahman
or Nirvana as the timeless principle in the soul is

---

[25]R. C. Zaehner, "Utopia and Beyond: Some
Indian Views," Eranos-Jahrbuch 32 (Zurich: Rhein
Verlag, 1964):293-96.

[26]The Gita doesn't form part of the sacred
Hindu canon. Nevertheless, it has won acceptance in
India as perhaps the greatest of all scriptures. It
is a turning point in Indian religious thought.
Zaehner notes: "It was the Gita that set in motion
the transformation of Hinduism from a mystical tech-
nique based on the ascetic virtues of renunciation
and self-forgetfulness into the impassioned religion
of self-abandonment to God, but the strictly religious impulse which gave momentum to the whole bhakti
movement stemmed from the Tamil lands of south
India." R. C. Zaehner, Hinduism (New York: Oxford
University Press, 1966), p. 134.

[27]Zaehner, Christianity and Other Religions,
pp. 140-41.

the prelude, subject to God's grace, to sharing in
the being of God himself who is the source of both
Brahman and Nirvana. The soul now realizes that the
infinite dimension it has experienced flows from the
indwelling of God. Realizing this it worships God
who is the source of its being and the Creator of
heaven and earth.

This is participation in the total being of
God rather than an achievement of an individual Nirvana. It is a step beyond the realization of one's
own higher soul as Brahman. Here, for the first time
in Hindu literature, the personal God makes it clear
that liberation from his purely human and material
condition is not the end of man's spiritual endeavor:
the end is a personal union with a personal God. If
contemplation is devoid of love of God, then contemplation of God's transcendence may be man's
spiritual goal. But if love is there, this cannot
fail to lead to union with the personal God Himself,
who is the ground from which Brahman itself proceeds.
Chapter fourteen of the Gita and especially eighteen
make it clear that only after the realization of the
soul as Brahman is it fit to receive the highest
love for God that leaves room for nothing else. God
wills that the perfected soul live in fellowship with
him in eternity as well as time. Thus Krishna's
final message has no longer anything to do with becoming Brahman. Rather it is a message that Christians have taken for granted but which came to the
Hindus with all the force of an amazing revelation,
the message that God loves man. No longer is a holy
indifference a supreme virtue nor is liberation in
isolation the supreme goal. Rather the goal is
union and communion with God in the bond of love.[28]

Ramanuja's commentary on the Gita confirms
this view. Ramanuja concedes that with liberation

---

[28]Zaehner, "Utopia and Beyond: Some Indian
Views," pp. 299-302. Of course there are other interpretations of the Gita. J. Gonda says that Bhakti
does not supplant "karma-yoga" and "jnana-yoga." It
represents an attempt to synthesize the three yogas
in an age when the distinctions between the personal
and impersonal aspect of the divinity were not so
neatly drawn. Cf. J. Gonda, Die Religionen Indiens
(Stuttgart: W. Kohlhammer Verlag, 1960), pp. 270-71.

one realizes oneness and eternity, but he insists
that the soul must be shaken out of passive contemplation of self and brought into the presence of
God, who is other than self, by means of a passion
of love. To realize the nature of one's immortal
soul as being unconditioned by time and space and to
see all things in the soul and the soul in all
things, is a godlike state. But this is not to
know God: to know God is to love him, which love
leads to union. In any form of mystical experience
from which love is absent, God is absent too.[29]
Ramanuja then, draws a quite clear distinction between God and Brahman or the Absolute which he
defines simply as the extra-temporal and extra-
spatial mode of existence in which the soul has its
being. This mode of existence it has in common with
God. But it is only an essential first stage free-
ing the soul for its encounter with God in love.[30]

Zaehner argues similarly from the twelfth
book of the Mahabharata which resembles the Gita in
that its description of liberation becomes increasingly theistic as the book moves to its close. As with
the Gita the teaching moves on from the mysticism of
man's eternal essence to that of the union of that
essence with God who is its ground. The isolation
of the soul is only a preliminary stage on the way
to union with God, and thus any system, including
the classical Samkhya, which makes no room for God,
must stand condemned.[31]

---

[29]Zaehner, Hindu and Muslim Mysticism, p. 85.

[30]Ibid., p. 188 and also Zaehner, Matter and
Spirit, pp. 113-20. This need not be interpreted,
though, as a movement from one attitude to another.
N. Smart notes: "What has happened is that Ramanuja
has stressed one side of the Upanishadic teaching and
Shankara another." Smart, The Yogi and the Devotee,
p. 124.

[31]Zaehner, "Utopia and Beyond: Some Indian
Views," pp. 302 and 308. Zaehner seems to give a
more cautious interpretation of the Mahabharata in
an article "Salvation in the Mahabharat," The Saviour
God, ed. S. G. F. Brandon (New York: Barnes and Noble,
1963), pp. 218-25. He writes: "What the relationship of the personal God to the Supreme Self is, however, is not made clear" (p. 221). And later: "It

Thus, faithfully following the message of the
Gita, expanding it and clarifying it, the 12th
book of India's great epic shows us how we must
distinguish between the Utopia of the soul in
its splendid isolation from the Utopia of union
with our source and ground in which, remaining
in some sense two we are yet one in that we are
both eternal, he because he is the source of
all things eternal as well as temporal, we because we share in his timeless being.[32]

Hinduism is mystical through and through,
and the radical reversal of the dominant trend especially in the Gita is therefore of overriding importance. It smashes the wall of elaborate self-
sufficiency that fallen man had built around himself
and brings him face to face with God. Taoism, Buddhism, and the Samkhya-Yoga are religions that opt
out of life, reject the world by rejecting individuality and the responsibilities that individuality
brings with it. Krishna comes to change all of that,
for he implies that though, theoretically, there may
be nothing wrong in this, it really amounts to a
colossal act of spiritual pride. It means that man,
by seeking to be like God in his eternal impassibil-
ity and unfathomable peace, spurns to be like God in
his capacity of creator and sustainer of the world.

Monism, then, would seem to be a perversion
of the natural hankering after unity and harmony
that is present in all men: it is mysticism's dead
end and rooted in original sin. It is to mistake
the human soul for the Eternal Himself. It is to
separate oneself not only from God but from one's
fellows.[33] This is not to be understood as an

_____

would be absurd to maintain that the didactic portions of the Mahabharata present any consistent view
of the nature of liberation . . . but it can be said
on the whole they tend to avoid the extremes of both
non-dualist Vedanta and the fully dualist Samkhya.
Their general tone, like that of the Upanishads can
only be described as 'pantheistic theism,'" p. 225.

[32]Zaehner, "Utopia and Beyond: Some Indian
Views," p. 309.

[33]Zaehner, Matter and Spirit, p. 129.

argument against Hinduism as such. Rather, Zaehner is arguing against one trend which he considers an aberration from the doctrine generally held by the main body of thought within that tradition.[34]

In Buddhism we also find that at times mysticism moves on from the ideal of the passionless peace of Nirvana to that of a living and loving relationship with a personal God. In Hinduism this is more evident than in Buddhism. But it is there in Buddhism too, for in the course of the centuries the Buddha who had never claimed to be more than a man became deified. And in the <u>Lotus of the True Law</u> the very ideal of nirvana is called in question. The realization of one's soul is the beginning of the way. It is love that brings the soul into the presence of the unknown God.[35] Through the influence of the Mahayanists, Nirvana is only a step on the way to enlightenment which consists in partaking in the nature of the celestial Buddha who is God. This progress beyond Nirvana is only possible by faith in the infinite grace of the Buddha leading to the perfect wisdom of Buddhahood.

In the Mahayana, Buddhism draws remarkably near to Christianity. Soul mysticism is sharply distinguished from the mysticism of the love of God, the former being considered inferior to the latter.

Zaehner's conclusion is that both the Gita and the Lotus Sutra have prepared India for hearing the good news that God had become man in Christ whose ultimate message was loving union with God. Christ comes to overcome the error that the soul of man in realizing its immortal and timeless "ground" thinks that it has attained the "groundless" godhead itself.

God, then, must become man both to show man his true nature which is a self giving love . . . and to show that the "transcendent self" too

---

[34]Zaehner, <u>Mysticism Sacred and Profane</u>, p. xv.

[35]R. C. Zaehner, "Can Mysticism be Christian?" New Blackfriars 41 (August 1960):28. Of course a Theravada Buddhist would not be convinced that this development through Mahayana Buddhism was valid.

must be crucified and immolated along with the
empirical self . . . in order that the spiritual
pride and self-sufficiency may be burnt out,
and that it may thus ascend into heaven to be
united forever with the Father in the love which
is the Holy Spirit through the self immolation
of the Incarnate Word, its own perfect exem-
plar.[36]

The other argument that Zaehner makes is
that Christ's life and teachings bring a perfection
to mysticism. His life, death and resurrection indicate a goal beyond Nirvana; the goal of the mystic
is not achieved until one arrives at loving union
with God.

The crucifixion of Christ is symbolic of
what transpires in the mystic. It is the total
giving of self: translated into Indian terms this
does not mean just giving up the "ego" and all love
of possessions--of "I" and mine as Buddhists say--
it means also the crucifixion of the eternal essence
which is the very ground of the soul and a final
refusal to accept a timeless beatitude apart from
God. In the passion of Christ God shows what love
means: it means to give up everything of oneself for
friend and enemy alike. By the example of the cross
each individual is summoned to deny himself that he
may find himself again in God. Individual consciousness breaks open to let in God's love and through
God the love of man, his image. Thus, mysticism
since the time of Christ, has taken on a new form
which emphasizes not only identity but also union
and communion. Christian mysticism, Hindu mysticism
initiated by the Gita, as well as what is most authentic in Islamic mysticism, is essentially an outpouring
of spirit and love.[37]

Mystically interpreted the crucifixion of
Christ represents not only the destruction of the
empirical self but of the transcendent one too, for
the image of God is still subject to spiritual pride,
and this too has to be slain. With the resurrection
the God image emerges finally purified, and with the

---

[36]Zaehner, Christianity and Other Religions,
p. 145.

[37]Zaehner, Matter and Spirit, pp. 198-203.

ascension the human soul, like the human soul of [38]
Christ, ascends to and is united with the Father.
Christ, having crucified the "ego," ascends to the
Father eternally united to Him through the force of
attraction called the Holy Spirit. This is an enactment of what the theistic mystics claim to experience.

> For by the cross was symbolized the essential
> relationship between the creature and its Crea-
> tor. The creature has no existence of its own:
> all it has it has from God; and only by re-
> storing its borrowed existence to its rightful
> Owner . . . can the proper relationship between
> Creator and creature be restored. Christ's
> sacrifice, the total sacrifice of what has been
> on loan, is the perfect exemplar of the sacri-
> fice that all men must make if they wish to
> share in the life of God, and not merely to en-
> joy the contemplation of their own soul.[39]

Such insight tells us something of man's
attitude towards God. But it can also give evidence
of God's attitude towards man. Zaehner reasons that
since Christ is God as well as man then the cross
shows us God as He really is: a perpetual giving of

---

[38]Zaehner, "Can Mysticism be Christian?"
p. 31. Zaehner also notes: "In Mysticism Sacred and
Profane I likened the Crucifixion to a parable of the
crucifixion of the ego and the rising from the ashes
of the ego of the immortal soul. I was wrong: for if
this were the whole message of the Cross to the Indian soul, it would be no fulfillment, for it would
merely re-enact in physical form a psychological
truth which was already well known. What the cross
does teach is what the Mahayana Buddhists instinc-
tively felt, namely, that the realization and isolation of the eternal essence of one's own soul is
simply a more subtle kind of selfishness which must
be purged away . . . this is the peace of the atman,
but it is not the peace that passeth all understanding." Zaehner, At Sundry Times, pp. 191-92.

[39]Zaehner, Mysticism Sacred and Profane,
p. 195.

Himself. It also shows that God takes the world
seriously. He even takes on death and suffering
that he may be one with us in all things. By the
cross Christ symbolizes the very life of the Godhead: the Son dying always to the Father and living
always and eternally in the Holy Spirit. Similarly
just as Christ's death and resurrection are a physical enactment of the spiritual reality of the
mystical experience, so is the mystical experience
itself the image of the life of God in His Trinity.
What Christ teaches, what the theistic mystic experiences is actually twofold: God's love for man;
man's loving response to God.[40]

Monism mistakes the individual human soul in
its timeless essence for the Godhead. It refuses
to concede that there can be relationships and diversity in the world. The doctrine of the Holy Trinity
might have been expressly revealed to refute this
error. If there are relationships within the Godhead itself, then surely there must be relationships
between God and the soul, and between one soul and
another. The Christian "myth" is the complete
antithesis to monism, for it is no more possible for
Christ to exist apart from the Father and the Holy
Spirit than it is for natural man to rid himself of
intellect and will.[41]

Of course, Zaehner has offered no conclusive
proof for this particular interpretation of Christ
and the mystical life. The monist might well object
that this is a theistic interpretation of the Christian tradition. Zaehner realizes that one does not
prove such assertions. His argument would go back
to what was said previously in chapter two concerning
Christ. In addition it fits in with his persuasions
concerning the "superiority" of theistic mysticism.
Thus his Christology and theism is not meant as a
bias. It is rather a conclusion of all that he has
argued concerning theistic mysticism.

We are faced then with two theories of mysticism (monism and theism) which are dogmatically as
different as they can be and just as the two dogmas

---

[40]Ibid., pp. 189-90.

[41]Zaehner, "Can Mysticism be Christian?"
p. 31.

differ entirely, so must the religious practices which derive from them. In the one case the object of self-realization can only be attained by a complete dissociation of the subjective self from the objective world. In the other the realization of God can be most directly attained by a life of prayer. "Of all the doctrinal differences that separate the different religions there appears to me to be one on which it is essential to take a stand-- the nature of God himself. It is a very real issue between theism on the one hand and either monism or pantheism on the other. Are we ourselves God or is He somebody or something other than ourselves. On this subject we have to choose either one or the other."[42]

Neither the monist nor the theist can give an absolute proof for choosing one dogma concerning God over another. Zaehner chooses the Christian conception in which God becomes incarnate in Christ because it restores to man a unity of being in his body and soul.

For the Hindus and Buddhists, with their belief in endless reincarnations, final death--the definitive extinction of all becoming and therefore of all life--could only mean a happy release and freedom of the spirit. Life is fraught with sorrow; death without rebirth is the ultimate release. This is true of all the mystics; the temptation of the mystic is, then, to exhalt death above life, for death means to be reunited with the eternal and timeless from which our miserable lives in time can only appear totally insignificant and unreal.

In Christianity, however, the balance is restored, for Christ did not only tell one to lose one's life He also demanded that we should make use of our talents. Surely the perfect formula for the ordering of our life in view of our death and our death in view of our life is Christ's command to die to self in order to yield a rich harvest of a worthwhile life fulfilled.[43]

---

[42]Zaehner, "Dogma," p. 17.

[43]Zaehner, Drugs, Mysticism, and Make-Believe, p. 185.

So, Zaehner once again returns to the argument that Christianity provides a "via media" for the religious aspirations of mankind. Through the Incarnation, he reasons, we are offered a perfect balance between "interior" (mystical) and exterior (prophetic) religions; between a mysticism that calls to life and one that calls to death. We see then a distinction between the prophetic vision of God on the one hand and the mystical experience of immortality on the other. The two can only meet in a specifically theistic mysticism which recognizes the absolute existence of God on the one hand and the separate and real existence of the creature on the other.[44]

---

[44]Zaehner, At Sundry Times, p. 178. "Of the monotheistic creeds it is only Christianity that builds a bridge between God, the Eternal, and man, the temporal, in the shape of Jesus the God-man, who in his dual nature is fully representative of both kinds of existence. Man is brought into relationship with God through Christ, who by his sacrifice on the cross, demonstrates God's love for man. At the same time God's grace produces in man a longing to share in the divine existence and love." Zaehner, Hindu and Muslim Mysticism, p. 86.

CHAPTER V

A CRITICAL EVALUATION OF ZAEHNER'S METHOD,

AND SOME ALTERNATIVE PROPOSALS

An Evaluation of Zaehner's Christological Arguments

As chapter two has shown, Zaehner has emphasized the importance of Christ's incarnation in inter-religious dialogue. The emphasis is well placed for in the Christian view one must come to terms with the meaning of Christ as Lord, Mediator, Saviour--the definitive revelation of God the Father. It would do no good to dissimulate these claims in the hope of easier harmony with other religions. A false picture of Christianity and its claims would only result.

Nevertheless, as Prof. H. D. Lewis so truly says, "the unique events narrated in the Gospels are the core of the Christian faith. These are not to be taken as mere symbols of something beyond them, whether in depths of our own experience, or in the absolute being of God. They are not just pictures but supreme reality. The Christian faith as a distinctive faith, cannot survive the surrender of particularity." In it the highest insights of Judaism, Islam Zoroastrianism, Hinduism and Buddhism have been realized, fulfilling alike the prophetic revelations and mystical knowledge of God, and of sacramental union with him in its transcendental and immanent aspects. Therefore, these basic elements being foundation truths must be held fast if Christianity is to retain its unique place and function in the history of religion . . . to discover the reality of Christ in all the religions of the world is the essence of the ecumenical approach.[1]

It is true that each major religion holds some particular teaching or myth as the central point of its belief. Each religion then is unique in the sense that it has a different central myth than any other religion. Zaehner rightly argues that Christianity's central myth is the incarnation of Christ; the human and the divine are joined. God becomes man in Jesus Christ.

Zaehner's affirmation of the uniqueness of the incarnation in religious history raises a preliminary question. Just what is proved when one argues uniqueness? All of the major religions claim uniqueness in one way or another. If they were not unique in some way they would have no reason to exist. That there are distinctive elements within religions could argue to the evident fact that there are differences between religions rather than argue to uniqueness as a basis of choosing one religion over another.

When one speaks of the "complete" revelation of God in Christ one can interpret "complete" in an exclusivist sense or in an open sense. For instance does one intend "complete" as I know it in my historical situation or "complete in history apart from any worshipper's value judgement"? One can be a Christian and maintain either opinion. A Christian need not maintain that every sort of human excellence is found in Christ, e.g., artistry. But this would not deny the Christian conviction that there is no deeper or fuller truth than in him. It is possible to believe this, and still approach the non-Christian religions with an open mind that has not rejected, on a priori grounds, the possibility that these religions may contribute to our knowledge of God, and that they may bring to light for us elements of the logos not detected in its historic manifestation.

Similarly we should not bandy the phrase "final revelation" as though we had a definite

---

[1] E. O. James, Christianity and Other Religions (London: Hodder & Stoughton, 1968), p. 191.

understanding of its meaning.[2] For example, does
it mean a once-for-all happening or a once-for-all
meaning concerning that which happened? How does
this meaning relate to my historical time? Since
revelation is incomplete without a recipient how can
any revelation be final until the subject receives
the revelation in his life and his time? Actually
the preceding questions have been posed simply to
show that a Christian need not hold an exclusivist
interpretation of revelation in Christ.[3] Even if
one holds an exclusivist interpretation he ought not
do so without admitting the difficulties connected
with his position. "Uniqueness is a common claim.
This is even found in religions that have no belief
in Incarnation; it is in orthodox Judaism which
holds that Moses was the chief of the prophets, and
even more in Islam which regards Muhammad as the
seal of the prophets, second only to God, sinless

---

[2]"The word 'finality' has come to be applied
to the Christian faith only during the last hundred
years. The term is not free from ambiguity. . . .
Finality does not mean exclusiveness or a negative
attitude towards genuine religious and moral experience elsewhere." Herbert Chadwick, "The Finality of the Christian Faith" in Lambert Essays on
Faith, ed. Archbishop of Canterbury (London: S.P.C.K.
Press, 1969), p. 22.

[3]John Macquarrie makes a similar observation
in commenting on the authority of Jesus. "The
Synoptic gospels stress the unique authority of the
Lord, but they could hardly be said to make an exclusive claim." John Macquarrie, "Christianity
and Other Faiths," Union Seminary Quarterly Review
20 (November 1964):40. For the idea that Christian
revelation is unique because of its content, but
which is unable to be proved cf. A. G. Hogg, "Christian Attitude to Non-Christian Faith," The Authority
of the Faith, ed. Wm. Paton (New York: International
Missionary Council, 1939), pp. 115-16. The author
argues that the content of revelation to which
Christianity bears witness must win conviction by
its own illuminating and renovating power. Its
acceptance as divine revelation cannot depend on
any proof.

and intercessor with God.[4]

How are we to speak about a "unique" and
"once-for-all" revelation in Christ? If this means
that God's active self-disclosing relationship to
men came to an end in Jesus Christ, it is difficult to accept. If God is one who sought repeatedly
to reveal himself to successive generations and centuries of men in Palestine; and if God is eternal
and universal as well as Living Being; then the
belief in a full and final revelation at one point
in history is open to serious question.

We may say, then, that the New Testament
understanding of the "once-for-all" character of
God's self-disclosure in Christ is best preserved
in terms of quality rather than spatial or chrono-
logical finality. And this seems to take us beyond
the either/or choice of kind versus degree of revelation, beyond the choice between special and general
revelation. The revelation in Christ was and is
once-for-all, decisive for those who have come to
know him. But who will presume to limit the divine
intent and power by saying that this revelation
cannot be partially reflected elsewhere, or that in
it lies the totality of truth without remainder?[5]

Professor Macquarrie has written along
similar lines observing that Christians are deluded
in thinking that their religion is superior to all
others and that their particular revelation is the
norm for other revelations. The notion of a normative revelation in the sense of an exclusive norm,
must be rejected as firmly as the notion of a uniquely true revelation. Yet one should not claim that
all religions are equally true and good.[6]

But, there are problems involved in this
incarnational belief. First of all, Christians themselves continue to dispute what they mean by saying

---

[4]Geoffrey Parrinder, Avatar and Incarnation
(London: Faber & Faber, 1970), p. 225.

[5]Gerald Cooke, As Christians Face Rival Religions (New York: Association Press, 1962), p. 168.

[6]Macquarrie, "Christianity and Other Faiths,"
pp. 39-44.

Jesus is the God-man. Unless Christians can produce a completer understanding of Incarnation they will enter the inter-religious dialogue presenting Christ confusedly or presenting their opinion as the interpretation of Christ. The non-Christian may well ask: "Which image of Christ am I to accept?" The question will be difficult to answer because the Christian will never explain or exhaust the mystery of Christ. Nevertheless, there is a need to interpret the mystery of Christ in the clearest way possible. This is a present crisis for Christian theology and Christology in particular. Until Christians have a clearer theological presentation of Christ they might be more cautious in proclaiming the Lordship of Christ, or salvation of all men in Christ as though these were totally understood realities. The Christian may continue to hold that God acted definitively, in a once-and-for-all fashion, in Jesus Christ; that in him alone human history and all cosmic evolution are redeemed. But merely stating this belief does not solve, for either the Christian or non-Christian, the problem of the needed reverent appreciation of other religions. Christ's mediatorship might well have to be understood in a more modest manner than in preceding centuries. Certainly any types of arrogance or absolutism will have to be avoided. This is not to say that Christians will surrender their convictions about the unique place of Christ within religious history. But it does say that in a new age the old Christology will appear inflated and tainted with a superiority complex. The Christian may have a personal conviction of Christ's supremacy. But he ought to admit that his conviction is not clear to, proved to, or shared by, non-Christians.

The Christology of Zaehner might well be faulted in this light. It might be termed "traditional" and pre-Vatican II. In the initial chapter of Concordant Discord Zaehner states plainly his dislike for modern Christian theology. He prefers an older and in his opinion more stable theology. In this he is mistaken, and runs the risk of a cavalier theology. In fact, of all the religions discussed Zaehner's presentation of Christianity seems the weakest. One may not ignore recent theological developments under the pretext that "there is nothing new under the sun." While being faithful to original sources, Christian theology, especially since the turn of the century, has significantly

influenced the Christian self-understanding.[7] To
ignore this theological influence necessitates
beginning the inter-religious dialogue from a false
starting-point. The Christian presentation of theology, and in particular for this case, Christology,
ought to begin from where it is presently, not where
it was. It is not enough to present the constant
conviction that Christ is the God-man. What the
Incarnation means, how it is understood now, by
ourselves and others, has been modified by theological research. To ignore this is to ignore the
Christian starting-point for dialogue.

The lack of precision in Zaehner's Christology is especially evident when he presents Christ
as the Logos of religious history. The clear cut
distinction which Zaehner makes between the incarnation of the Logos and the Spirit allows him to consider Jesus as the founder of Christianity while the
Holy Spirit is the universal spirit who gives life
to all religions. This permits him to maintain both
his concrete Catholic identity and his Catholic universality. The problem with this is that even
Catholic theology does not allow for this neat
separation of Christ/Spirit. As one works out more
fully the meaning of "the Spirit of Christ" the
distinction and subsequent attribution of different
roles to Christ/Spirit become more difficult to
maintain.

In addition to this, Zaehner's use of the
Logos as a principle of interpretation and fulfillment for other religions is used too casually. The
oriental is said to be meeting a personal God
through Jesus Christ. Christ unites full interiority
and absolute transcendency. He fulfills the deepest
non-Christian intuitions. Since God in Christ has
affected all humanity and history, history is now
sacred history. The incarnate Logos then leads to
interpreting other religions in the light. What is
objectionable in this analysis is that one can be so
confident that he understands the way the logos is

---

[7]For Zaehner's dislike of modern theology cf.
Zaehner, Concordant Discord, pp. 15-20. Part of his
attitude stems from a desire and an ability to interpret various religions primarily through their
scriptures rather than the present lived experience
of these religions.

working.

R. D. Young comments on this facile use of the logos when he says:

> There is too quick a desire to bring everything under the umbrella of the logos. Everything becomes grist for the Christian religion in a way that denies dialogue and must anger adherents of other religions. There is also the assumption that the logos, because it has associations with reason, is a completely manageable item, and that faith has given access to its secret. . . . Much the same criticism could be leveled at R. C. Zaehner. Zaehner sees God revealed "at sundry times and in divers manners" not only in the Old Testament, but in other cultures too. . . . Zaehner concludes that it is in Christianity that the highest insights of both the Hindus and the Buddhists are fulfilled. Again, the question is raised as to how the logos is known so clearly that it can be the criterion of judgement.[8]

One can also raise a question concerning Zaehner's choice of items to be compared. Why choose one element that has similarities with Christianity and see its fulfillment in Christianity while ignoring dissimilar elements, e.g., Nirvana, that have no apparent fulfillment in Christianity? Presumably, Christian elements would be the basis of choice, but this, of course, is a presupposition in favor of Christianity. There is a further question as to how certain elements in various religions that are claimed to be part of the logos structure actually pertain to the totality of the religion involved. Are they vital elements? How do they condition the entirety of the religion of which they are a part? In other words are the comparisons made on important points and a fair basis?

One of the main arguments used by Zaehner is that Christ is the fulfillment of religious aspirations of mankind. The arguments that Zaehner uses

---

[8]Robert D. Young, Encounter with World Religions (Philadelphia: Westminster Press, 1970), pp. 75-76.

are not without value; they are valuable points in favor of Christ and his teaching. But the arguments do not substantiate the "fulfillment" claim to the satisfaction of non-Christians. In this light the fulfillment model should not be used in inter-religious dialogue since as G. Parrinder remarks "it smacks of patronage."[9]

One also experiences difficulty in arguing that a religion, e.g., Hinduism is a preparation for the gospel. The Hindu might well argue that the gospel is only an explication of what Hinduism already contained. Rather than Hinduism vaguely foreshadowing the gospel, the gospel would merely elaborate basically Hindu tenets. In this way the gospel would add nothing substantially new to Hinduism. Zaehner even uses this kind of argument in relation to Islam which, he says, adds nothing really new to Christianity even though it arose hundreds of years after Christianity.[10]

---

[9]There is an additional difficulty of even knowing which interpretation to use. "This approach (fulfillment theory) has a certain meaning in recognizing the fact that there is a universal aspiration and yearning towards the truth and ultimate existence. But there is a question, as some of the exponents of the theory of fulfillment indicate, to consider the fulfillment as a straight extension of the prepared line of elevation. There must be a radical departure from the way in order to have renewal in Christ. Repentance and confession are indispensable in accepting the revealing event in Jesus Christ." Masao Takenaka, "Christian Encounter with Men of Non-Christian Faiths in Japan," Harvard Divinity Bulletin 27:3 (1963):15-16. H. H. Farmer has also pointed out what he considers acceptable and non-acceptable fulfillment theories. H. H. Farmer, "The Authority of the Faith,"The Authority of the Faith, ed. Wm. Paton (New York: International Missionary Council, 1939), pp. 151-55.

[10]Professor Geoffrey Parrinder feels that to speak of other religions as preparations for the gospel is no longer a worthwhile approach to dialogue. There are so many things that don't prepare for Christianity at all. Re-incarnation is such an example. Yet there is something to be said for it since it is a fact of life for so many

Zaehner argues that Christ blended together
into one the mystical and prophetic traditions thereby fulfilling the totality of man's religious
desires. It is true that Christ's message has a
certain universal appeal. But what of Mahayana Buddhism, neo-Confucianism, the reformed Hinduism of
Gandhi and Tagore, which Zaehner himself says unite
these mystical and prophetic traditions in themselves? Even Islam could be included in this
category if Sufism is considered as an integral part
of Islam. Their message strikes a balance between
the prophetic and mystical traditions. The further
presupposition here is that the most desirable religion is a blend of the two traditions. A Theravada
Buddhist would not be so easily convinced. His
answer might well be that the highest spirituality
can be realized in the intensification of one tradition, i.e., the mystical tradition. Islam or Judaism
might well argue for the intensification of the
prophetic tradition.

Zaehner has also argued that Christ is a
pre-eminent religious figure because He is the center of man's mind and the center of man's quest for
solidarity. This argument will appear to be true--
to the Christian. In faith the Christian can accept
Christ as a personal and communal center. To the
non-Christian the argument will not be convincing
for Zaehner argues that Jesus is the Logos supplying
to the human race the coherence it had lost. Once
again the problem is the identification of Christ
with a universally acceptable Logos.

The fulfillment theme is also applied to the
intensity of Christ's command to love. The universal
love that Christ taught and lived has won universal
admiration. One could even argue that this teaching

---

non-Christians, and has been so for thousands of
years--whatever its truthfulness may be. What must
be avoided is making elements of other religions
only subservient to Christianity. The arguments
for preparation and fulfillment may make sense from
the Christian theological viewpoint. From the viewpoint of Eastern religions it will be different.
Perhaps we will have to consider the unknown Krishna
of Christianity. Geoffrey Parrinder, private interview at King's College, London, May 1972.

on love is found nowhere else, in its scope, in religious history.[11] It does much to make Christ universally accepted as an authentic religious teacher. The difficulty, of course, is in showing that Christ's teaching on love is really a fulfillment of a previous teaching such as the Gita. Does the Hindu acceptance of the Gita bind one to see God's hand at work preparing for the incarnation in Jesus Christ? Again, from the perspective of Christian faith, it may appear so. Outside of this perspective the preparation and fulfillment is far more difficult to discern. In fact, outside of this perspective one has to ask whether or not the emphasis on love as a preeminent virtue is one more western, Christian, presupposition in dialogue.

Zaehner has also argued that Christ's Incarnation has had a decisive influence on the union of matter and spirit, reconciling the two, as well as reconciling the temporal and the eternal, and God and man. Once again though, the arguments are based on a Christian presupposition. As is well known there is no agreement between East and West on the meaning of matter and man's relation to it. Is bliss to be found in detachment from matter, including the body, or does one achieve oneself fully through the use of

---

[11]Cf., for example, the chapter of comparison between the Buddhist concept of compassion and the Christian concept of love in Henri de Lubac, Aspects of Buddhism (New York: Sheed & Ward, 1954). Nevertheless, Zaehner makes it clear that the specialness of Christian love is not a conclusive argument. "Yet Christian ethics is not what makes Christianity unique, for the ethics of self-denial had already been preached by the Buddha, who, no less than Christ taught a universal charity that should comprise all mankind, including our enemies. What makes Christianity what it is, as St. Paul clearly saw, is the scandal and foolishness of the cross, the doctrine of atonement by bloody human sacrifice and the resurrection of the body." Zaehner, At Sundry Times, p. 181. For an opinion stressing the normative value of sacrificial love in religious dialogue, cf. Antonio Gualtieri, "Confessional Theology in the Context of the History of Religions," Studies in Religion, 1:4 (1972):353-55.

matter, including the body? The question is basic because it influences so many other questions associated with it. It comes down to a question of how one sees the world, man, his goal and purpose. And Zaehner himself has mentioned that neither view of itself can be proved. If one's presupposition is Eastern then, of course, much of Zaehner's argumentation will be unconvincing. This is merely to state once again a basic impasse between two modes of thought.

This is not to say that the line of argumentation that Zaehner used is completely without value. It is more and more accepted that the traditional Indian view of matter needs some corrective. This acceptance has come from Indian thinkers such as Sri Aurobindo, Hiriyanna and Radhakrishnan. Of course none of these thinkers have felt compelled to accept Christ as a unique incarnate figure, nor to leave Hinduism to embrace Christianity. They have learned from Christianity just as Christians have learned from Hinduism.

A further observation should also be made here. What Zaehner considers a balanced view on matter, body, and man stems from the Incarnation and in particular his interpretation of Christ's death and resurrection. This was particularly stressed in the contrast between resurrection of the body and Nirvana. However sensible the resurrection may appear to the Christian, he should be reminded that this central Christian teaching can only be accepted in faith. The Indian mind may accept this as a Christian teaching but this is quite different from accepting it as a reality that truly changes one's outlook on life and matter. Ultimately the Hindu, for example, would become a Christian if he were to accept the reality of the resurrection of Christ. In short, this is to say that Zaehner's argument concerning the resurrection will not be convincing outside of a Christian context. One cannot begin a dialogue by asking the other to accept a faith conviction. It would be an unfair presupposition.

Part of Zaehner's argumentation about Christ comes from a comparison with other major religious figures. Not all the points of comparison need be discussed here. But certain evaluations should be made to indicate the delicacy of such comparisons.

It is necessary to avoid invidious comparisons or
attitudes of superiority.

First of all, the doctrine of Incarnation
does not fit easily into all forms of Hinduism. The
fully monistic philosophers are uneasy with the
Avatar portions of the Gita, and needless to say with
Christian Incarnation. Secondly, many Hindus would
accept Christ as an Avatar, but not as a once-and-
for-all incarnation.[12] The difference between the
two types of divine intervention is significant. The
Hindu can do little more than accept Christ simply
as an Avatar. The Christian would feel that this
does not do justice to Christ's Incarnation. Yet,
once again, since the Incarnation is ultimately
affirmed in faith, it will not be convincing to one
who does not share that faith. Nor will the Hindu
see a fulfillment of his religion in Christ's Incarnation. At most it will appear as a greater
emphasizing of a religious attitude already contained in Hinduism.

Contemporary philosophical Hinduism holds
that the ultimate reality, Brahman, is beyond all
qualities, including personality, and that personal
deities, such as the Jahweh of the Bible or the

---

[12]In the Christian-Hindu dialogue the differences between Avatar and Incarnation should be
carefully noted. The Christian does not help inter-
religious dialogue by calling Christ an Avatar.
Rather, it confuses the situation. "It is a serious
mistake to introduce Christ as an 'Avatar,' but then
add that he is the only and exclusive Avatar. That
for the Hindu is unacceptable--a limitation of the
freedom of God who adopts any form when and where he
pleases. In Indian theology there must be many avatars. If Christ is an avatar he cannot be the only
one! What has to be stressed is that the knowledge
of Christ is of the nature of Brahmavidya. Christ
is unique in the same sense as Brahman is unique--
has to be unique, not in the sense of one among the
avatars who may claim pre-eminence. Knowledge of
Christ requires no less spirituality than Brahmavidya." Charles Davis, review of Klaus Klostermaier,
Hindu and Christian in Vrindaban (London: S. C. M.
Press, 1969), in Studies in Religion 3:1, 82.

Krishna of the Gita, are partial images of the absolute created for the benefit of that majority of
mankind who cannot rise above anthropomorphic thinking to the pure absolute. Thus the various religions
of the world, with their different proportions of
anthropomorphism and mysticism, can be seen as so
many approaches to the truth that is fully revealed
in the Upanishads.[13]

Zaehner's argumentation would seem to agree
with Professor Parrinder who has studied the inter-
religious implications of Incarnation in his book
Avatar and Incarnation. Like Zaehner, Parrinder sees
a specificity and even a uniqueness in the Incarnation which is different from the Hindu concept of
Avatar. One criterion of distinction is the historical nature of the Incarnation. Parrinder (and
Zaehner) question whether or not an avatar is a real
incarnation in the flesh, an inhistorization of the
deity. Ultimately avatar cannot be equated with Incarnation. History is the sphere of the singular,
the unique. The uniqueness of the Incarnation comes
from its being fully historical. In regard to
singularity Christian theology goes not speak of
many avatars, but rather one Incarnation, "once for
all." "The uniqueness of Christ is seen first in
his singularity as an individual historical man;
much more in his identification with the sole messiah who plays the central role in the establishment
of the kingdom of God; but chiefly in his death and
resurrection. In these latter ways Christ is quite
different from any other religious figure."[14]

Despite such assertions one has to acknowledge their inconclusiveness. The importance of the
historical nature of the Incarnation might well
appeal to the western or Christian attitude. But it

---

[13]John Hick, "The Christian View of Other
Faiths," Expository Times, 84:2, 37-38.

[14]Parrinder, Avatar and Incarnation, p. 221.
In addition to questioning the historicity of Krishna Zaehner wonders about the foibles of Krishna.
Zaehner argues that such deficiencies are irrecon-
cilable with an authentic God-man manifestation. To
call Krishna God would allow frivolity in God.

is a presupposition not shared by all other religions. As Professor Huston Smith has noted the Hindu response to some religious reality is not "did it happen" but rather "what does it mean?"[15] Even Professor Parrinder notices the difficulty involved in the historical incarnational argument. He writes: "For Hinduism, the humanity of Jesus is especially important, though it should be distinguished from historicity. The historical sense has been weak in Hindu tradition and to insist first of all upon a Christian understanding of history is to invite disappointment and misunderstanding. True appreciation of history can begin with the man Jesus Christ."[16]

Zaehner's comparison of Christ with Buddha is also problematic. The claim for Christ is that he was divine as well as human. The claim can only be made for Buddha contrary to his own wishes, a "divinization" which began hundreds of years after his death. Yet, an argument for the pre-eminence of a divine-human person will not go far in the face of orthodox Buddhist agnosticism.

One of the few comparisons made by Zaehner between Buddha's teaching and Christ's concerns Nirvana as contrasted with eternal life. But here again what comparison is conclusive without clarifying the presuppositions about man, life and purpose? The dead-end that Zaehner sees in Buddha's view of life and Nirvana seem deficient to Zaehner. But wouldn't Zaehner's view seem exaggerated to a Buddhist? Further than this, Zaehner would better have to evidence why he chooses this as a point of comparison and not another. Could not the Buddhist choose a comparison which would leave his own position

---

[15]"One can generate little interest in India over whether Hindu myths are 'true' in our Western sense--whether Krishna really lived, for example. The accounts are true to the needs of the human spirit, and what could be more important?" Huston Smith, "Accents of the World's Religions" in Comparative Religion, ed. John Bowman (Leiden: E. J. Brill, 1972), p. 18.

[16]Parrinder, Avatar and Incarnation, p. 278.

seemingly stronger? Commenting on differences between Buddhist and Christian views towards goals and
salvation, R. Panikkar notes:

> Buddhism offers a different attitude. It does
> not want to uncondition but de-condition man;
> it is not concerned with reaching transcendence,
> but with overcoming immanence; it does not care
> as much about God as about de-conditioning man
> in a radical and ultimate way. Man has to cease
> to be what he is, not in order to become another
> thing, not even God, but in order to negate
> totally the human and worldly situation. Bud-
> dhism shatters the human dream of any type of
> imaginable or thinkable survival.[17]

A somewhat similar approach is used in comparing Christ and Muhammad. Muhammad was only
"divinized" by some Muslims in later generations.
It can be mentioned that Muhammad was not of the
moral stature of Christ since Muhammad's foibles are
well known. But Muhammad no more would have accepted divinization than he would have accepted
Christ as true God. Respect could be given to
Christ but there is only one God Allah. Zaehner
insists that the distortion of the Father physic-
ally generating the Son be clarified. But even if
this is understood Muhammad could not accept Christ
as equal to God Himself.

Of course Zaehner can argue that the difficulty of comparing these religious figures with
Christ, the difficulty of accepting the surpassing
value of Jesus Christ by other religions, is indicative of just that point which he is arguing.
There ought to be difficulty in accepting the incarnation because it is not central to religions other
than Christianity. Zaehner's argument is that
variations of incarnations have arisen inexorably in
religions in spite of the founders' contrary desires.
This urge toward incarnation is for Zaehner the
coherent pattern of the major world religions. What

---

[17]Raymundo Panikkar, "Sunyata and Pleroma:
The Buddhist and Christian Response to the Human Pre-
dicament," Religion and the Humanizing of Man, ed.
J. M. Robinson (Ontario: Riverside Color Press,
1972), p. 79.

is peripheral in the other religions is constitutive of Christianity. Naturally, there will be difficulty in accepting a total notion of incarnation. Nevertheless, this movement towards incarnation is, in Zaehner's view, the preparation which finds fulfillment in Jesus Christ. Once again, one's viewpoint will depend on one's interpretation. When asked: "Is Hinduism a praeparatio evangelica?" Zaehner replied: "The preparation is there but whether they accept the conclusion is something different, they don't. . . ."[18]

What we have done thus far in this chapter is evaluate Zaehner's interpretation of Christ among the other world religions. On the one hand there has been an attempt to show the value in Zaehner's arguments and method. On the other hand the evaluation has been cautionary. The arguments are debatable since non-Christians and even some Christians find points of disagreement. In addition some arguments contain Christian presuppositions which are unacceptable to non-Christians. Zaehner at times admits that some of his arguments only appear evident from a Christian viewpoint. This would pertain especially to the incarnation and fulfillment model. The note of caution will remind us that Zaehner's arguments for Christ and the other religions are not, and perhaps cannot be, probative. Some people may be convinced by this kind of argumentation. It may also have a special value for Christians. But its value in inter-religious dialogue is limited.

An Evaluation of Zaehner's Ecclesiological Arguments

As we saw previously, Zaehner employs the fulfillment model in relation to Christ and the other major religions. He uses this same model in relation to the Church and other major world religions. Accordingly, similar strengths and weaknesses of argumentation for Christ will re-appear in connection with the Church.

---

[18]R. C. Zaehner, private interview at All Souls College, Oxford, May 1972.

Zaehner's basic argument is that the church is a fulfillment of man's religious desire for unity and convergence. He argues that the church offers a structure in which mankind can find an individual and collective unity. Because of Christ and his teaching the church has, as no other structure, the potential to unify mankind in a common religious brotherhood.

Even this attitude raises an initial problem. Can we presume that the desire for unity is shared by all, or at least shared in the same way? The present plurality of religions responds to varying religious cultural expressions. Religious stagnation is avoided to some degree by the challenge that one religion offers to another. And there is a possibility of stagnation if one envisages future unity based on a conversion to one of the presently existing religions. As we have seen, Zaehner does not propose a stereotyped model of a church for future religious unity. For him unity will be based on an interplay of religions leading somehow to a convergence in Christ.[19] Our caution though is that unity may not be presumed a priori. And if we do accept a convergence of religions, the type of unity envisaged will have to be worked out clearly, and probably slowly, to avoid the impression that dialogue is only a subtle means to produce conversion of one religion to another.

(Zaehner) seems to assume that technological man will prefer a religion defined in terms of an organizational purpose in history. One would have to grant that in the first stages of the technological revolution this did seem to be the trend, but there are suggestions in the attitudes of research scientists and men in the forefront of the communications revolution that history is less and less their basic frame of reference and organizational structures very seldom their basic form of expression.[20]

---

[19]For a discussion of recent literature on the topic of "convergence" cf. William Cenker, "The Convergence of Religions," Cross Currents 22:4, 429-37.

[20]Paul Younger, review of R. C. Zaehner,

Zaehner's argument of the church as a <u>via</u> <u>media</u> for religious groups also seems unconvincing in the last analysis. It may be argued that the church offers a balanced approach to the religious life of man. As Zaehner indicates much of the church's strength comes from its ability to blend the prophetic and mystical traditions, materialism with interiority, corporate and individual salvation, the transcendent and the immanent. As attractive as this ideal may appear one has to wonder why all religions should see this balanced religion as desirable. Certain religious traditions choose one religious pole to the exclusion of the opposite pole because it is thought that in the former resides the fullest religious truth. For example, the Theravada Buddhist sees no need personally to choose a religious structure that emphasizes the prophetic tradition. For him the highest truth is the interior, mystical quest. To claim that this emphasis is deficient, as Zaehner does, would be one more indication for the Theravadin that the Christian has not yet appreciated the liberating value of interiority.

Perhaps the greatest deficiency of all with the Church being a center of unity or convergence for mankind is that it is admittedly an ideal center. Zaehner candidly discusses the difference between the church as it is and the church as it ought to be. Herein lies the problem. The unifying possibilities of the church for mankind are just that: possibilities. The balanced, unifying model of the church is largely a theoretical conception. Zaehner admits that the ideal church may not exist for hundreds or thousands of years to come, if it ever comes.

This ideal has limited value in the present inter-religious dialogue. To propose the Church as a unifying center is to propose a religion that still needs and will continue to need, purification. In its present state the Church does not evidence sufficient universality to embrace all the religious strivings of men.

As Professor William Neil has noted:

To say that no other religion has the same

Matter and Spirit in Theology Today, October 1966, p. 438.

potentialities as a world-wide faith for every
man is neither to denigrate the God-given truth
in Buddhism, Islam and the rest, nor to say that
at this stage Christianity as generally prac-
tised and understood in the west presents much
more than a caricature of its purpose.

Perhaps the best corrective to hasty judgement is
to measure these 2000 years against the untold
millions of years of man's development. Organized Christianity is still in its infancy, as in
the mind of man as he seeks to grapple with
truths that could only come to him by revelation. The half has not yet been told and the
full implications for human thought and action
of the coming of God in Christ have as yet been
only dimly grasped by most of us.[21]

What Zaehner proposes is some far distant
ideal of Christianity that is too distant from
reality to usefully serve present inter-religious
dialogue. To speak of the church as a center, but
which may never be realized on earth, is to add a
hindrance to the dialogue of the present time. For
practical purposes talk of conversion to the Church
as center might be best discarded.

We believe that Christ is the ultimate fulfillment of all religion, the final and definitive
word of God but the same cannot be said of
Christianity. Christianity, as an organized
religion suffers from the same defects as other
religions. . . . As it developed in history it
is predominantly western religion, lacking many
of the deeper insights of eastern religion. We
have to face the fact that, in the concrete,
Hinduism and Buddhism are in many respects better religions than our current Catholicism or
any form of western Christianity. For a devout
and educated Hindu or Buddhist to become a
Christian would often mean a descent and not an
ascent in the scale of spiritual life. He
would often meet with a philosophy less profound,
a spirituality less demanding, a piety less intense, a morality less pure. In most cases it

---

[21]E. O. James, Christianity and Other Religions, from the editor's Preface by Wm. Neil, pp. 5-6.

131

would mean the loss of all the treasures of wisdom and grace which he had known in his own religious tradition.[22]

Until the mystery of Christ has been pre- sented to non-Christians in terms which are meaning- ful to them in the light of their own religious tradition, there is no reason to suppose that God wills the conversion of these people to other reli- gions. Christians may try to show that the fullness of the world's religious treasures are found in Christ. But merely to convert non-Christians to the present imperfect Christian system of religion would serve little purpose. Zaehner mentions that he is not interested in converting people. A meet- ing of religions would be preferable in which each religion would bring its own insight and richness. Through this Christ will be revealed as Supreme Wisdom and Savior. But this may only take place at the end of time.

This is not to say that Zaehner's vision of the Church is without value. We are merely question- ing its practical, ecumenical value. Zaehner has argued that because of its constitution and teaching the Church alone possesses the structure for unifica- tion that man desires. Perhaps this is true. Perhaps the Church is also the most universal of possible structures for the future. The present inter-religious dialogue ought to consider such structures and claims seriously. But as Zaehner himself indicates this new church, i.e., the future church needs the contribution of the religions of the world. Without this contribution the church will remain provincial. With it a new unifying center will emerge. Whether or not this new church will resemble our present church or will continue to be called the Christian Church remains to be seen. Nevertheless, this kind of creation is a future pos- sibility. Its possibility may depend on a present willingness to avoid any narrow ecclesial approach.

Some Alternate Proposals for Dialogue

Up to this point we have evaluated Zaehner's

---

[22]Bede Griffiths, "Erroneous Beliefs and Un- authorized Rites," London Tablet, 14 April 1973, p.24.

understanding of both Christ and the Church as it pertains to the dialogue among religions. There are advantages but also major drawbacks to the model of dialogue that he offers. At this point then, we should consider a possibly more helpful approach. This approach is partially based on the insight of a contemporary religious writer, Professor Raymundo Panikkar. On the other hand, it is also based on the implications of some of the insights of Professor Zaehner while also trying to avoid some of the deficiencies of his fulfillment model.

We begin by underlining the importance of seeing Christ in relation to the other religions outside of an exclusively semitic context. Can we, in any possible way, understand the experience of the other man, his culture or his religion, in order to incorporate it into our personal horizon? Can we understand a text which has emerged out of another context, unless we share in that context, or in a wider horizon which includes that context? In other words, have we the right to speak for the whole of mankind if our horizon is not that of the whole humanity? This is a recognition that the realm within which Christ's universality was conceived and affirmed covers no longer the whole horizon of human experience. One could then recognize a certain legitimate claim to universality inasmuch as the context was assumed to be the universal texture. On the other hand, one could deny any actual universality because the world, i.e., the range of human experience, subjective and objective, has radically changed since the times in which the Christian doctrine was formulated, and can no longer be simply identified with the Christian context.

This does not mean that Christians can no longer speak of Christ as a universal saviour. Nor does it mean that the particularist texts of scripture regarding Jesus as unique saviour are without value. Rather we are cautioned against interpretations which need not be held in the name of Christianity. As W. C. Smith has noted:

> I do not see the need of an image that would reduce Christian truth to a part of some larger whole. Liberal universalism and an absolutist interpretation are in constant interplay. The point is to deny that one has to choose between orthodoxy and liberalism, between loyalty to

one's own faith in all its fulness, and loyalty
to other men's faith in all its variety. An ef-
fete and watered-down eclecticism that is sub-
stituted for christian orthodoxy and for other
men's orthodoxy is no final solution. A truly
Christian attitude to outsiders must involve
both the validity of Christian orthodoxy and an
acceptance of men of other orthodoxies as one's
brothers--in one's own eyes, and in the eyes of
God. In this way . . . truth lies not in an
either/or, but in a both/and.[23]

In an essay on the meaning of the name of
Christ as expressing that mystery which transcends
all names R. Panikkar notes:

Any name belongs to a particular language and in
this language it has its proper meaning. To
affirm that a certain name has a universal validity involves the affirmation that a particular
worldview from which the name originates has a
universal validity. This, in point of fact, was
the underlying assumption on more than one occasion in the history of religions. In the
present world's religious and human constella-
tion such an assumption seems untenable.[24]

Panikkar says this to emphasize that the
biblical affirmations need proper translation and
interpretation when applied outside of the semitic
cultural world.

One must also emphasize the insufficiency of
speaking of Jesus only in spatio-temporal terms. No
Christian will say that the living Jesus of his
faith is only a being of the past. The Christian
speaks of the cosmic Christ who exceeds spatio-
temporal coordinates. This is an important emphasis
if one wants to see Christ outside of the confines
of the semitic world. This is an emphasis, moreover,
that Zaehner makes especially when he espouses

---

[23]W. C. Smith, The Faith of Other Men (New
York: The New American Library, 1963), pp. 79-80.

[24]Raymundo Panikkar, "Salvation in Christ;
Concreteness and Universality the Supername" unpub-
lished book draft, University of California at Santa
Barbara, 1972, p. 21.

Teilhard de Chardin's writings.

If Jesus is to be understood then, as being unique saviour, in a way which does justice to the experience of the other peoples of the world and to the deepest Christian insights, he cannot be linked with the biblical tradition exclusively. That the message of the bible is experienced as valid by Christians does not imply that it must be the only message. The basic function of the bible is not to carry a thought-out, speculative, or even cultural message, but to witness to a historical fact; that out of the people of Israel was born Jesus in whom the fullness of the Godhead dwelt in a corporeal manner.

In trying to get a balanced biblical view of Jesus, in emphasizing Jesus who transcends time, space, and cultural determinants, we are saying in effect that the unique, salvific role of Jesus Christ cannot be approached as an 'objective' religious fact. A subjective knowledge of Jesus Christ is required to give meaning to his title of "Lord and Saviour," i.e., he must also be my Saviour.

The identity of Christ that we are looking for is not that which we may expect from accurate historical information or a physical analysis of his body, nor simply what a philosophical scrutiny of his words and doctrines may yield concerning who he is. Rather, we are looking for that identity which is found in the encounter with a person. We are looking for that knowledge which springs up when we really know and love somebody, which is more than, and different from, the results of all the examinations of the objective data.

This personal knowledge, in this case of the person of Jesus, is an important emphasis in Christology. It emphasizes the need to know Christ in faith as a saviour without which he remains merely an objectified symbol of salvation. It is the difference between identity and identification in regard to Jesus Christ. In the former case he is truly known as saviour. What makes Jesus truly Jesus is his personal identity which can only be said to be real and thus true if we enter into a personal relationship with him. Only then may one discover the living Christ of faith who lives in the interior of oneself. Panikkar asks that we do not confound personal identity with personal identification. The latter means the identification of a person by means of external marks of identification which, properly speaking do not belong to the person. It responds to the question "what." Personal identity, on the other hand, refers to the core of the human being present to oneself and to others; it means that which makes the person his own self. Personal identity is that which responds to the question "who?" and it is expressed by the authentic "I" which is only real when involved in a network of personal relationships. Personal identity enables one to answer the question of the "who" because it has discovered the who within oneself. In other words, only in faith can we have a personal relationship with Jesus and discover his personal identity. This is far different from personal identification which would discover him as a great man in history, but without any living relationship to him. When one knows the personal identity of Jesus one can know him as Lord and Saviour.

This implies that the word "Jesus" has two basically different meanings: one as a historical category and another as a personal category. The former is reached by means of historical identification which permits us to speak about Jesus and the beliefs Christians have in him. The latter is reached by means of personal identity and allows us to discover him as a part of our personal being. The Jesus of the Christian believer is the risen Lord, in whatever way one may care to interpret the resurrection. He is not simply the historical Jesus but the risen one, a Jesus who as a person enters into the very structure of our own personal existence. He cannot be discovered in the exclusively outer world of history, nor in the exclusively inner world of our thoughts, feelings or beliefs.[25]

This attitude is present also in W. C. Smith: "Rather than saying that Jesus Christ is the full revelation of God, I would say that he is the revelation of God to me, and has not been to many others. . . . He continues to reveal and be more true than before, and more truly for some than

---

[25]Ibid., p. 40.

others."[26]

It is also found in Zaehner when he writes a-
bout his personal entrance into the Catholic Church:
"I have freely accepted the 'bondage' of the Catholic
Church, and I would scarcely have done this if I had
not thought that this was in fact the true religion
--for me. This does not mean that I am particularly
anxious to go around converting people, because I
am not at all convinced that Catholic Christianity
need be the true religion for everyone else."[27]

We are not trying to dismiss a central Christian conviction. Rather, we are looking for an
acceptance of the statement: Christ is the unique
saviour in a way that need not be exclusivistic and
monopolistic. "There is no other name granted to man
by which they may receive salvation."[28] This name
may be less particular and more common than one ordinarily imagines, or even the New Testament ordinarily
imagines. Jesus is not the revealed name, but he
reveals the Supername. The name stands for the
reality expressed by that name. It is not the magic
of the name that saves, but the reality expressed
by that name. The task of every human being is finding the Name.

> There is one, eternal, infinite, transcendent
> wisdom or Truth, which has been revealing itself
> to man from the beginning of history. It is
> this one Truth which is the source of all
> genuine religion. But this Truth transcends
> all words and all thought. It cannot properly
> be named or expressed. Every religion seeks
> to express this one Truth by means of signs and
> symbols in the form of beliefs and rituals and
> paths of ascetic and moral life. In all alike
> the divine Wisdom is at work, shaping the evolu-
> tion of humanity. Each religion through its
> system of symbols offers a unique insight into
> the divine mystery which is the object of all

---

[26]W. C. Smith, Questions of Religious Truth
(New York: Scribner & Sons, 1967), p. 91.

[27]Zaehner, Concordant Discord, p. 17.

[28]Acts of the Apostles 4:12 (N.E.B.).

religious belief.[29]

　　　To say that "Jesus" is the universal Saviour
means that there is universal salvation, but that the
Saviour is not merely a historical figure nor simply
a revealer of religious facts. Salvation--whatever
it may consist of--always involves a personal act,
thus a personal experience and a personal encounter.
This is said to emphasize that it is in the Spirit
that man encounters his saviour; and yet for the
Christian the encounter is not disassociated from
the historical manifestation of Christ's saving
mystery. The normal way for the Christian will be
through revelation of the saving name by Jesus, whom
the Christian believes is risen. But the Christian
will not deny a priori that this meeting, experience
or conviction may take any other form. He will be
convinced for himself that the mystery with which he
is in communion through Jesus is the mystery which
saves, giving meaning to existence, hope to living,
and love to reality, to any being capable of experiencing the same through as many forms as there may
be. The expression personal encounter intends to
avoid the purely subjective feeling as much as the
merely objective and doctrinal approach. Personal
experience is not merely sentimental or subjective
discovery of another being.

　　　When one affirms, then, that "Jesus is Lord"
one affirms that one's being is not exhausted in an
isolated private self nor in any equalitarian hori-
zontal relation with similar selves. Rather it
affirms the need of a Lord who opens up for me the
ultimate horizon where my person can exist. It
means, further, that this Lord, whose Lordship can
take many forms, has taken for me an ultimate form
which is indissolubly connected with Jesus of
Nazareth.

　　　The committed Christian may declare that the
revelation in Christ is unique because of the incom-
parable depth of God's concern and love which he
finds there. Christ is irreplaceable for the Christian. It is conceivable that God has not revealed
these aspects of his nature elsewhere so clearly and
dramatically. It is also conceivable that a God of
such character would disclose authentically something

---

[29]Griffiths, "Erroneous Beliefs," p. 24.

of himself in other cultures of mankind. All that
a Christian can say is what is involved in his own
Christian commitment, and that as yet he has found
no equal of Jesus Christ in non-Christian faiths;
he cannot know whether this corresponds to a fact in
the objective order of things or whether it reflects
his too preliminary acquaintance with other religions.[30] Thus, what we have been emphasizing is the
importance of a subjective acceptance of Jesus
Christ as saviour. In viewing the relationship
between Christ and the believer we have an indication of Christ as universal saviour. To see Christ
as an object results in a false perspective.

> The Lord who saves is not an independent dis-
> connected force unrelated to me, so that he can
> choose to save me or any other. He is not an
> object. . . . What I mean to say is that the
> process of salvation is not an extrinsic process
> nor an automatic event we can bring about with
> our individual capacity alone. When the Lord
> saves me, when he discloses reality to me, he
> does it not to a private individual, but to
> the whole world, mirroring microcosmically the
> macrocosmic process.[31]

These preceding considerations concerning
Christ will perhaps show that we need not be restricted to a narrow Christological understanding
when one considers inter-religious dialogue. Since
Zaehner discusses the church as well as Christ we
can look now at a view of the church which avoids
provincialism and offers hope for genuine dialogue
in equality between religious men. This view, in
one way, goes beyond Zaehner's church-fulfillment
model. In another way it is based on one of Zaehner's important, but unfortunately undeveloped remarks. "We can only look forward in faith to the day
when all men will be as living stones, built up, in
a spiritual house acceptable to God by Jesus Christ.
And it will be not only our house but the house of
all those who from all the religions of the world
may one day see fit to pour their spiritual

---

[30]Cooke, As Christians Face Rival Religions,
pp. 168-69.

[31]Panikkar, "Salvation in Christ, pp. 77.

treasures into it."[32]

We should be warned against using other religions by interpreting them only through Christian concepts. This would ultimately absolutize Christianity to the point of seeing its truth as exclusively saving. The New Testament itself seems to tend toward the exclusive interpretation in favor of Christianity, but this is offset to some degree by some other texts. Furthermore, it is possible to see the exclusivist texts as hortatory exhortations to conversion rather than universal, metaphysical affirmations. Historical Christianity should not be equated with trans-historical truth. Certainly Christianity has more than a historical message, i.e., it contains a value which transcends history. But the question remains whether we are judging one religion from inside of it and the other from outside. Viewed from the inside in faith and commitment one sees the concrete universality of that religion. An outside view does not see the link between the two because it looks only upon objectified values. The comparison is not only unfair but also no religion is totally objectifiable. It is legitimate to interpret another religion in the light of your own for the purpose of understanding or clarification. But one ought not to start with this as an a priori position that this interpretation is the way for the dialogue to proceed. Such a position begs the question from the beginning.

We are not affirming that what Christ conveyed is the same or not the same as the message of Hinduism. We are making, however, a fundamental assumption. The ultimate religious fact does not lie exclusively in the realm of doctrine or even of individual self-consciousness and therefore it can—and well may—be present everywhere and in every religion, although its explicitation may require varied degrees of discovery, realization, evangelization, revelation, hermeneutics, etc. And this makes it plausible that this very fundamental religious fact may have different names, interpretations, levels of consciousness and the like, which are not irrelevant, but which for the person undergoing the concrete process of realization, may be equivalent.

---

[32] Zaehner, <u>Christianity and Other Religions</u>, p. 148.

Once again we note W. C. Smith's observation.

> On the whole there has been a tendency to hold
> that, the Christian faith being true, it must
> follow logically that other faiths are there-
> fore false. The logic is simply not cogent.
>
> The fallacy stems from confusing faith with
> theology, in one or other of its various forms.
> Since the conclusion conflicts with the faith
> itself, I infer that the theology used as
> premise must mis-represent its own master. I
> predict that a time will come perhaps fairly
> soon, when men will see rather that if the
> Christian revelation is valid, then it follows
> from this very fact that other men's faith is
> genuine, is the form through which God encoun-
> ters those other men, and saves them.[33]

We are pleading for a dekerygmatization of
faith. The kerygma has its place, as has also myth,
within any religion, but the "proclamation of the
message" should not be identified without qualifica-
tions with the reality that religions aim at
disclosing. We should apply this in a very special
manner to Christianity and also say that our
reason for this is a conviction that the living and
ultimately real Christ is not exclusively the
kerygma of the Lord, but the Lord Himself.

Can we not say that there is a primordial
theandric fact, which appears in a certain fullness
in Jesus, but which is manifested and at work everywhere? This is the mystery which exists since the
beginning of time and which will only appear in the
end of time in its fullness. It is disheartening,
and not consonant with experience, to monopolize
that mystery and make of it the private property of
Christians only.[34]

The conviction that Jesus Christ represents
the summit of Christian awareness cannot be assumed

---

[33]Smith, The Faith of Other Men, p. 92.

[34]Raymundo Panikkar, "Category of Growth in
Comparative Religion: A Critical Self-Examination,"
Harvard Theological Review 66 (January 1973):115-16.

at the very outset of dialogue. To recognize in
Jesus the cosmic Christ, the mediator, the universal
principle, the logos, could be said to be the unique
distinctive and fundamental feature of the Christian
proclamation, but we cannot start there where, if
at all, one should end. Jesus represents the historical incarnation of that Mystery which, hidden
but yet present through the ages, transcends history,
and, of course, Judaism and Christianity also.[35]

May we say, for instance, that Isvara is
performing, within a certain sector of Hinduism, what
Christ also stands for, and that what the followers
of both religions existentially and really are aiming
at is equivalent? Could this not be part of a universal Christology which would make room for different theologies and also different religions? One
can have an internal and authentic religious experience in more than one existing religious tradition,
without betraying either. In commenting on this
approach of Panikkar, R. D. Young notes:

> For him, (Panikkar) "The Church" must not be
> identified with outer appearance, nor "the sacra-
> ments" identified with Baptism and the Lord's
> supper. The sacraments may be the ordinary means
> by which God leads the people of earth to himself.
> But there is a broader vision to be maintained.
> Christ is not only the historical redeemer, but
> the second person of the Trinity--the only one,
> ontological, temporal, and eternal link between
> God and the world. If Baptism and the Lord's
> supper have the support of the historical Christ,
> and are thus connected with the will of God,
> could it be that there are other sacraments that
> are supported by the eternal Christ and the
> Triune God? Panikkar poses the question and
> answers it affirmatively, in his words, "The
> good bonafide Hindu is saved by Christ, not by
> Hinduism--but it is through the sacraments of
> Hinduism."[36]

And in a similar vein of observation Professor C. J. Bleeker has noted:

---

[35] Ibid., p. 126.

[36] Young, Encounter with World Religions,
p. 181.

We are justified or even obliged to believe that
God has lighted the path to truth for all peoples
in all ages. The non-Christian religions owe
their existence to this fact. The inscrutability
of God's wisdom does not permit us to comprehend
the purpose that lies behind what we consider to
be the essentially different kinds of knowledge
of God found in the world religions. At most we
can speak of a pluriformal dispensation of the
truth which must be meaningful because comparative studies demonstrate that the various types
of religions have close ideological ties with
one another. Indeed, we may say that the religions of the world represent spiritual concep-
tions of human existence that are complementary
to each other.[37]

Neither the use of another tradition to enrich one's own nor the interpretation of one religion
in the light of another is adequate or appropriate
for the theological task and religious needs of our
times. Rather the category for religious encounter
and development of religion (and religions) is growth.

Growth means continuity and development, but
also implies transformation and revolution. How
Hinduism has to grow, or Christianity or other religions, we do not yet know fully.

In the modern world some voices are suggesting
that all mankind must learn to see religious
diversity in a way that we may construct on
earth an englobing concord and fellowship that
recognizes differences and even contrasts in
the religious realms as parts within an harmonious circle of world-wide human community--
the truth lying not with one element in the
complex but in the adjustment of each to the
others.[38]

---

[37]C. J. Bleeker, Christ in Modern Athens
(Leiden: E. J. Brill, 1965), pp. 122-23.

[38]Smith, The Faith of Other Men,p. 79.

142

Conclusion

We have finally come to a point where we can make some concluding remarks which will perhaps explicitate the previous reflections and evaluations.

Much of Zaehner's argumentation has dealt with other religions as preparations for the gospel, and Christianity as their fulfillment. In this he is not alone since many other Catholic and Protestant authors hold basically similar positions.[39] This is to say that much Christian thinking on this issue has not gone beyond the preparation/fulfillment model. We have tried to indicate that this is not a satisfactory solution to the present dialogue among religions of the world. On the other hand the argumentation is not completely without value. Zaehner's argument that the Incarnation is a unique blending of the divine and human, that the Incarnation is the coherent pattern to which other religions point, in some ways, is to be taken seriously by all religions. The Incarnation's influence on the importance of

---

[39]This is basically the method that the Catholic Church used at the Second Vatican Council when discussing the relationship between Catholicism and Non-Christian religions. In a survey article on what German Protestant theologians are saying on this topic Paul Knitter notes their overall negative view. All of the theologians studied call for dialogue. But owing to their view of justification or the unique salvific role of Christ they either practically deny or severely limit the possibility of salvation in or through other religions. Other religions may prepare for Christ, they may amount to a searching for salvation, they do not have real answers which bring salvation. The author concludes that this basis precludes effective dialogue with the non-Christian world. Paul Knitter, "What is German Protestant Theology Saying About the Non-Christian Religions?" Neue Zeitschrift für Systematische Theologie und Religionsphilosophie 15:1 (1973):38-64.

matter, on the importance of history[40] should cause
special reflection on the part of Hinduism and Buddhism. Thus Zaehner has not tried to dissimulate
any of the Christian claims in the name of a false
irenicism. But we have had to conclude that there
is no single conclusive argument that proves
Zaehner's assertions. Even if his arguments are
taken cumulatively they are not probative, nor does
Zaehner intend them to be "proofs." As we have indicated before the presuppositions of each religion
preclude such arguments as proofs. It is not only a
question of pre-suppositions. It is also necessary
to realize that the full appreciation of the Incarnation comes when one accepts it in faith, when one
accepts Jesus Christ as his personal Lord.[41] Of
course, this faith context cannot be imposed on
other participants of the dialogue from the outset.
Hence, the fulfillment in Christ model of dialogue
may be valuable for a Christian self-understanding
of the role of Christ in universal religious history.
This is the way Christians see it from the vantage
point of their faith and conviction. But as a basis

----

[40]This once again would raise the presupposition of the role and importance of history in
religion. It should also be a reminder that the
Christians themselves are not unanimous in relation
to the meaning or importance of history.

[41]Arguing against the Barthian depreciation
of 'religion' H. R. Niebuhr claims a type of uniqueness for the Christian religion. But this uniqueness
is predicated upon a Christian context and a subjective appreciation, i.e., how it appears to the
Christian. "I recognize that henceforth all time
for me will be informed and conformed and reformed
by the image of Christ. In this sense my religion
as a Christian confessor is both unique and final;
it is unique in the sense that of all mankind there
is only one man in history who understands and makes
me understand my religion, my bondage to God. And
it is final, because Christ is a totally concrete
man who leaves no region of soul or mind unillumined,
unsearched, and uncriticized." H. Richard Niebuhr,
"Religion and the Finality of Christ," Harvard
Divinity Bulletin 26:3 (1963):30.

of dialogue, as a basis of inter-religious growth,
it is bound to be too limited and to appear too
Christian a solution. The possibilities explored
in the latter part of this concluding chapter would
appear to offer a more viable approach to the dialogue among world religions.

In a similar way we have seen that the fulfillment arguments as applied to the Christian Church
are not totally satisfactory. Again, there is something to be said for the universal character of the
Christian Church as well as the fact of the Christ
who is its unifying center. As a vision and a theory this may give all religions cause for reflection.
But we have noted the practical difficulties involved in this attitude, the too Western character
of the Christian Church as it exists today. The fulfillment argument in relation to the Church seems
to be a fruitless way of engaging in dialogue today.
Perhaps the most helpful insight that Zaehner has
offered in relation to the Church is his view of a
future "church" into which all the religions of the
world will contribute their richness. This is not a
type of crass synthesis which Zaehner explicitly
rejects. It is rather a possibility of growing together towards a future unity which in the Christian
view may be the future community willed by God.

As for the future religious dialogue there
are many possible approaches. But based on what we
have seen thus far there are at least several elements, among many others, which the Christian ought
to keep in mind. First of all, we might do well to
evaluate non-Christian religions from as positive a
viewpoint as possible. The realm of grace is not to
be equated exclusively with the historical event of
Jesus Christ. God speaks his gracious word in many
and various ways. One may receive grace without
explicitly knowing Jesus, and one may spurn grace
without having heard the gospel. The Christian may
continue to use Jesus as the criterion of divine
grace, but ought to acknowledge that God's gracious
approach to mankind is restricted neither to Jesus'
historical existence nor to that of the church. It
can be maintained that the diverse religious traditions do function, in their own ways, to create a
self in which God is present. God, who wills the
salvation of all men, raises up inspired men and
communities to create patterns of religious belief,

practice, and worship that are relevant to the particular historical and cultural situations in which different peoples live, and in which they must achieve reconciliation with God and their brothers. Religious studies in the future may well give more thought to how people may be converted to the sacred in the context of their own life. The diverse religious faiths may be caused, at least in part, by God's specific redemptive action. This implies that the present religious pluralism may well be willed by God as part of his mysterious plan for the salvation of all men.

Secondly, a word of caution concerning the role of religious truth in the future dialogue. Much emphasis has been given to a conceptual view of truth, as ought to be the case. But too much emphasis can be placed here as though it is the only criterion for truth. A more functional approach may also be helpful. It is possible that one tradition may possess more advanced beliefs, cults, and institutions that more accurately represent the divine-human reality and relation than another tradition. On the other hand, given the situation of the world today, an ethical approach to dialogue should not be overlooked. One of the great needs of our time is a spirituality that gives meaning and purpose to man's existence, no matter what tradition it may come from. Theology in the context of world religions may well remind us that religions are not themselves the primary objects of faith. They rather function to induce and express the believer's lived understanding of himself as he apprehends reality and value. This is a plea for the importance of man to live spiritually, with a sense of the transcendent, and not only with a refined theology. As Professor Dewick has noted: "The Christian apologist must meet the non-Christian claims, not only with theological or philosophical arguments, but also with evidence that Christianity does in fact produce on the whole better men and women than any other religion."[42] To establish such

---

[42] E. C. Dewick, The Christian Attitude to Other Religions: Hulsean Lectures, 1949 (Cambridge: The University Press, 1953), p. 49. This is not meant to claim that such evidence is in fact available. It is a recognition of the importance of ethical and spiritual elements in religious dialogue.

criteria, be they love or peace or sharing, etc.,
is not an easy task. Nor are they the only ways or
even the best ways to religious truth. But a tradition that can offer answers to authentic existence
will certainly be looked upon as a community where
God is at work. It will be a community that is
coming to terms with the existential question of
divine truth, i.e., the reality of God's renewing
presence in the life of the believer.

A third element will be the category which
was previously mentioned as 'growth.' Each tradition must discern how it can enrich and be enriched
by other traditions. This is not a call to eclecticism or leveling off traditions at the lowest
common demoninator. It is rather a recognition
that if the world is headed towards a future pattern
of unity, then in a changed context the parochial
traditions of another day may no longer function to
mediate the sacred. Together mankind will be called
upon to create a new religious tradition that is
compatible with the emerging cultural situation in
which mankind will seek to love meaningfully and
peaceably. For the Christian, already committed to
the Incarnational principle, this could represent a
new creation, a new occasion, to allow God to be
fully present in and to humanity. This new
'church' will not only express the faith and religious quest of men living in the world, but will
also serve God as a means of his continuing advent
into mankind's history. In some ways this will
appear as only a generalized theory. On the other
hand, it is the practical attitude that must moti-
vate men of religious traditions when they meet in
dialogue as brothers and equals.

Finally, we should repeat that the Christian
and other religions men are not required to abandon
the claims to revelational truth that they have perceived and experienced in their tradition. In
understanding the beliefs of others one may find
that there are teachings that can not be accepted
as fully as one's own. In the present religious
situation this problem may arise quite often. But
what we can sacrifice is an exclusivist understanding of revelation that restricts divine disclosure
to one's own particular tradition. The Christian
ought to admit that he has no monopoly over Jesus
Christ or the ways in which he brings about salvation
--a salvation that has always been referred to as a

147

mystery. The theandric principle may have a special connection with the Incarnate Jesus Christ, but it is also manifested in a variety of ways. And again it must be remembered that the Christian appreciation of Jesus Christ is mediated by faith. This gives the Christian the conviction of the Lordship of Jesus Christ but does not give him the right to impose this faith conviction as a presupposition of religious dialogue.

This entire study has not provided a solution from the Christian viewpoint of how religious dialogue should progress. It has indicated some pitfalls and some possibly fruitful attitudinal approaches. The future goal is not clearly seen and at times seems impossible of attainment. But we must leave room in this work for God to produce the impossible. Let religious men bring together their intelligence, their spirituality, and willingness to search together. Then we shall see how we grow and where God leads.

SELECTED BIBLIOGRAPHY

Primary Sources

Books

Zaehner, R. C. Foolishness to the Greeks: An In-
       augural Lecture Delivered Before the Univer-
       sity of Oxford, Nov. 1953. Oxford: Clarendon
       Press, 1953.

_____. Zurvan, A Zoroastrian Dilemma. London:
       Oxford University Press, 1955.

_____. "The Religious Instinct." The New Outline
       of Modern Knowledge. Edited by A. Pryce-
       Jones. London: Victor Gollancz, 1956.

_____. The Teaching of the Magi. London: Oxford
       University Press, 1956.

_____. Mysticism, Sacred and Profane: An Inquiry
       into Some Varieties of Praeternatural Ex-
       perience. London: Oxford University Press,
       1957.

_____. At Sundry Times: An Essay in the Compari-
       son of Religions. The Evans Lectures 1957.
       London: Faber and Faber, 1958.

_____. Hindu and Muslim Mysticism. The Jordan
       Lectures 1959. London: Athlone Press, 1960.

_____. The Dawn and Twilight of Zoroastrianism.
       London: Weidenfeld and Nicolson, 1961.

_____. Hinduism. London: Oxford University Press,
       1962.

_____. Matter and Spirit: Their Convergence in
       Eastern Religions, Marx and de Chardin. New
       York: Harper and Row, 1963.

_____. "Salvation in the Mahabharat." The Saviour
God. Edited by S. G. F. Brandon. New York:
Barnes and Noble, 1963.

_____. Christianity and Other Religions. Vol. 146
of the Twentieth Century Encyclopedia of
Catholicism. Edited by Henri Daniel-Rops.
150 vols. New York: Hawthorne Press, 1964.

_____. "Conclusion." Concise Encyclopedia of
Living Faiths. Edited by R. C. Zaehner.
London: Oxford University Press, 1964.

_____. The Bhagavad-Gita: With a Commentary Based
on the Original Sources. London: Oxford University Press, 1969.

_____. Concordant Discord: The Interdependence of
Faiths: Being the Gifford Lectures delivered
at St. Andrews in 1967-1969. London: Oxford
University Press, 1970.

_____. Dialectical Christianity and Christian
Materialism. Being the Riddell Memorial
Lectures for 1969. London: Oxford University
Press, 1971.

_____. Evolution in Religion: A Study in Sri
Aurobindo and Pierre Teilhard de Chardin.
London: Oxford University Press, 1971.

_____. Drugs, Mysticism, and Make-Believe. Lon-
don: Collins and Co., 1972.

_____. Our Savage God: The Perverse Use of
Eastern Thought. New York: Sheed and Ward,
1974.

Articles

Zaehner, R. C. "Menace of Mescalin." Blackfriars
35 (July-August 1954):310-23.

_____. "Dogma." The Hibbert Journal 53 (October
1954):9-18.

_____. "Islam and Christ." Dublin Review 231:474
(1957):271-88.

_____. "Nirvana." The Hibbert Journal 57 (January 1959):117-25.

_____. "Christianity and the World Religions." Blackfriars 41 (August 1960):256-71.

_____. "The Idea of God in Hinduism." Jubilee 11 (May 1963):37-40.

_____. "Christianity and Marxism." Jubilee 11 (August 1963):8-11.

_____. "Can Mysticism Be Christian?" New Blackfriars 46 (October 1964):21-31.

_____. "Theology, Drugs, and Zen." Theology 74:613 (1971):291-97.

_____. "The Other God." Theology 74:614 (1971):350-56.

_____. "Salvation Through Death." Theology 74:615 (1971):391-98.

_____. "Learning from Other Faiths: 1. Hinduism." Expository Times 83:6 (1972):164-68.

_____. "Mysticism Without Love." Religious Studies 10:3 (1974):257-64.

_____. "Why Not Islam?" Religious Studies 11:2 (1975):167-79.

Secondary Sources

Books

Allen, E. L. Christianity Among the Religions. London: Allen and Unwin, 1960.

Anderson, J. N. D. Christianity and Comparative Religion. Illinois: Inter-Varsity Press, 1970.

Ashby, Philip. History and the Future of Religious Thought. New Jersey: Prentice-Hall, 1963.

Baird, R. D. Category Formation and the History of Religions. The Hague: Mouton, 1971.

Berry, Thomas. Five Oriental Philosophies. Albany: Magi Books, 1968.

Bianchi, Ugo, and Bleecker, C.J., eds. Problems and Methods of the History of Religions. Leiden: E. J. Brill, 1972.

Bleeker, C. J. Christ in Modern Athens. Leiden: E. J. Brill, 1965.

_____. The Sacred Bridge: Researches into the Nature and Structure of Religion. Leiden: E. J. Brill, 1963.

Bouquet, A. C. The Christian Faith and Non-Christian Religions. London: Nisbet, 1958.

Chadwick, Herbert. "The Finality of the Christian Faith." Lambert Essays on Faith. Edited by Archbishop of Canterbury. London: S.P.C.K. Press, 1969.

Chethimattam, John. Consciousness and Reality. Bangalore: The Bangalore Press, 1967.

Cooke, Gerald. As Christians Face Rival Religions. New York: Association Press, 1962.

Cornelis, Ernst. Valeurs chrétiennes des religions non-chrétiennes: Histoire du salut et histoire des religions: Christianisme et Bouddhisme. Paris: Cerf, 1965.

Cragg, Kenneth. Christianity in World Perspective. London: Lutterworth, 1968.

Cuttat, Jacques. Expérience chrétienne et spiritualité orientale. Paris and New York: Desclée, 1967.

Davis, Charles. Christ and the World Religions. New York: Herder & Herder, 1971.

Derrick, Christopher. Light of Revelation and Non-Christians. New York: St. Paul's Editions, 1965.

Dewick, E. C. The Christian Attitude to Other Religions: Hulsean Lectures, 1949. Cambridge: The University Press, 1953.

Dhanis, E. L'Eglise et les religions. Rome: Gregorian University Press, 1966.

Farmer, Herbert H. "The Authority of the Faith." The Authority of the Faith. Edited by Wm. Paton. New York: International Missionary Council, 1939.

_____. Revelation and Religion: Studies in the Theological Interpretation of Religious Types. London: Nisbet, 1954.

Farquhar, J. N. The Crown of Hinduism. London: Oxford University Press, 1930.

Girault, René. Evangile et religions aujourd'hui. Paris: Les Editions Ouvrieres, 1969.

Gonda, J. Die Religionen Indiens. Vol. 1. Stuttgart: W. Kohlhammer Verlag, 1960.

Graham, Aelred. The End of Religion. New York: Harcourt Brace Jovanovich, 1971.

Griffiths, Bede. "The Meeting of East and West." Light of Revelation and Non-Christians. Edited by Christopher Derrick. New York: St. Paul's Editions, 1965.

_____. Vedanta and Christian Faith. Los Angeles: Dawn Horse Press, 1973.

Hallencreutz, Carl. New Approaches to Men of Other Faiths: 1938-1968, A Theological Discussion. Hitchin, Herts.: Wm. Carling and Co., 1969.

Hogg, A. G. "Christian Attitude to Non-Christian Faith." The Authority of the Faith. Edited by Wm. Paton. New York: International Missionary Council, 1939.

James, E. O. Christianity and Other Religions. London: Hodder and Stoughton, 1968.

Jung, Moses, and Nikhilananda, Swami. Relations Among Religions Today: A Handbook of Policies and Principles. Leiden: E. J. Brill, 1963.

Jurji, E. J., ed. Religious Pluralism and World Community. Leiden: E. J. Brill, 1969.

Kitagawa, J. M., ed. The History of Religions. Vol. 1: Essays in Divinity. Edited by J. M. Kitagawa. 6 vols. Chicago: Chicago University Press, 1967.

_____. "The History of Religious Subjectivity." The History of Religions: Essays in Methodology. Edited by Mircea Eliade and J. M. Kitagawa. Chicago: University of Chicago Press, 1959.

_____. Understanding and Believing: Essays by Joachim Wach. New York: Harper & Row, 1968.

Klostermaier, Klaus. In the Paradise of Krishna: Hindu and Christian Seekers. Philadelphia: Westminster Press, 1969.

Kraemer, Hendrik. Why Christianity of All Religions? London: Lutterworth, 1962.

Kristensen, W. B. The Meaning of Religion: Lectures in the Phenomenology of Religion. The Hague: Martinus Nijhoff, 1960.

Leeuwen, Arend van. Christianity in World History: The Meeting of the Faiths of East and West. London: Edinburgh House Press, 1964.

Lewis, H. D., and Slater, R. L. World Religions: Meeting Points and Major Issues. London: Watts, 1966.

Lubac, Henri de. Aspects of Buddhism. New York: Sheed and Ward, 1954.

Masters, R. E. L., and Houston, Jean. The Varieties of Psychedelic Experience. New York: Holt, Rinehart and Winston, 1966.

McKain, David. Christianity: Some Non-Christian Appraisals. New York: McGraw-Hill, 1964.

Munson, Thomas. Reflective Theology: Philosophical
    Orientations in Religion. New Haven: Yale
    University Press, 1968.

Neill, Stephen. Christian Faith and Other Faiths:
    The Christian Dialogue with Other Religions.
    London: Oxford University Press, 1961.

Neuner, Joseph, ed. Christian Revelation and World
    Religions. London: Burns and Oates, 1967.

Newbigin, Lesslie. A Faith for This One World?
    London: SCM Press, 1961.

_____. The Finality of Christ. London: SCM
    Press, 1969.

_____. Trinitarian Faith and Today's Mission.
    Virginia: John Knox Press, 1964.

Panikkar, Raymundo. Salvation in Christ: Concrete-
    ness and Universality, the Supername. Cali-
    fornia: University of California at Santa
    Barbara, 1972.

_____. "Sunyata and Pleroma: The Buddhist and
    Christian Response to the Human Predicament."
    Religion and the Humanizing of Man. Edited
    by J. M. Robinson. Ontario: Riverside Color
    Press, 1972.

_____. The Unknown Christ of Hinduism. London:
    Darton, Longman and Todd, 1961.

_____. "The Ways of West and East." New Dimensions
    in Religious Experience. Proceedings of the
    College Theology Society. Edited by George
    Devine. Staten Island, N.Y.: Alba House,
    1971.

Parrinder, Geoffrey. Avatar and Incarnation. Lon-
    don: Faber & Faber, 1970.

_____. The Christian Debate: Light from the East.
    New York: Doubleday & Co., 1968.

_____. "The Place of Jesus Christ in World Reli-
    gions." Christ For Us Today. Edited by Nor-
    man Pittinger. London: SCM Press, 1968.

Roper, Anita. The Anonymous Christian. New York:
Sheed and Ward, 1966.

Rouner, Leroy S., ed. Philosophy, Religion, and the
Coming World Civilization: Essays in Honor
of W. E. Hocking. The Hague: Martinus Nijhoff, 1966.

Schlette, Heinz. Towards a Theology of Religions.
New York: Herder & Herder, 1966.

Slater, Robert L. World Religions and World Community. New York: Columbia University Press,
1963.

Smart, Ninian. A Dialogue of Religions. London:
SCM Press, 1960.

_____. The Science of Religion and the Sociology
of Knowledge: Some Methodological Questions.
New Jersey: Princeton University Press, 1973.

_____. The Yogi and the Devotee. The Interplay
Between the Upanishads and Catholic Theology.
London: Allen and Unwin, 1968.

Smith, Huston. "Accents of the World's Religions."
Comparative Religion. Edited by John Bowman.
Leiden: E. J. Brill, 1972.

Smith, W. C. The Faith of Other Men. New York: New
American Library, 1963.

_____. The Meaning and End of Religion. New York:
Macmillan, 1963.

_____. Questions of Religious Truth. New York:
Scribner and Sons, 1967.

Straelen, H. van. The Catholic Encounter with World
Religions. London: Burns and Oates, 1966.

Thils, Gustav. Propos et problèmes de la théologie
des religions non-chrétiennes. Tournai:
Casterman, 1966.

Thomas, Owen, ed. Attitudes Towards Other Religions.
Some Christian Interpretations. New York:
Harper and Row, 1969.

Tillich, Paul. Christianity and the Encounter of
    World Religions. New York: Columbia Univer-
    sity Press, 1963.

Toynbee, Arnold. An Historian's Approach to Reli-
    gion. New York: Scribner, 1956.

Visser't Hooft, W. A. No Other Name: The Choice
    Between Syncretism and Christian Universal-
    ism. Philadelphia: Westminster Press, 1963.

White, John, ed. The Highest States of Conscious-
    ness. New York: Doubleday and Co., 1972.

Whitson, Robley. The Coming Convergence of World
    Religions. New York: Newman Press, 1971.

Widengren, George. "An Introduction to the Pheno-
    menology of Religion." Ways of Understanding
    Religion. Edited by Wm. Capps. New York:
    Macmillan, 1972.

_____. Liber Amicorum: Studies in Honor of Prof.
    C. J. Bleeker. Leiden: E. J. Brill, 1969.

Young, Robert D. Encounter with World Religions.
    Philadelphia: Westminster Press, 1970.

Articles

Baum, Gregory. "Christianity and Other Religions:
    A Catholic Problem." Cross Currents 16 (Fall
    1966):447-62.

_____. "Religion in Contemporary Roman Catholic
    Theology." Journal of Religious Thought 26:2
    (1969):41-56.

Benz, Ernst. "Christianity and Other Religions in a
    Changing World Situation." Journal of Church
    and State 11 (Spring 1969):205-19.

Bouquet, A. C. "Christian Faith and Non-Christian
    Religions." Modern Churchman 10 (October
    1966):92-104.

Bowker, J. W. "Can Differences Make a Difference?
    A Comment on Tillich's Proposals for Dialogue

Between Religions." The Journal of Theological Studies 24 (April 1973):158-88.

Braden, C. S. "Christian Encounter with World Religions." Journal of Church Studies 7 (Autumn 1965):388-402.

Caster, Marcel van. "Christianity Confronted by Religious Pluralism." Lumen Vitae 21 (December 1966):529-42.

Cenker, William. "The Convergence of Religions." Cross Currents 22:4 (1973):429-37.

Clarke, Norris. "The Self in Eastern and Western Thought." International Philosophical Quarterly 6:1 (1966):101-109.

Clasper, Paul D. "Buddhism and Christianity in the Light of God's Revelation in Christ." South East Asia Journal of Theology 3 (July 1961): 8-18.

Copeland, E. L. "Christian Dialogue with Major World Religions." Review and Expositor 68 (Winter 1971):53-64.

Cragg, Kenneth. "Encounter with Non-Christian Faiths." Union Seminary Quarterly Review 19 (May 1964):299-309.

Danielou, Jean. "Non-Christians and Christ." The Month 223 (March 1967):137-52.

Easton, W. B., Jr. "Christ's Atonement and the Non-Christian." Theology Today 20 (April 1963): 61-75.

Ernst, Cornelius. "World Religions and Christian Theology." New Blackfriars 50 (October and November 1969):693-99 and 731-36.

Griffiths, Bede. "Erroneous Beliefs and Unauthorized Rites." The Tablet (London), 14 April 1973, p. 24.

Gualtieri, Antonio. "Confessional Theology in the Context of the History of Religions." Studies in Religion 1:4 (1972):347-60.

_____. "Descriptive and Evaluative Formulae for Comparative Religion." Theological Studies 29 (March 1968):52-71.

Hashimoto, H. "Christian Theology and the Challenge of Non-Christian Religions." Journal of Biblical Religion 28 (July 1960):299-307.

Hick, John. "The Christian View of Other Faiths." Expository Times 83:2 (1972):36-39.

Hillman, Eugene. "The Missionary Idea Today." American Ecclesiastical Review 145 (April 1971):242-56.

Hoffman, R. "Development of Mission Theology in the Twentieth Century." Theological Studies 23 (Summer 1962):419-41.

Klostermaier, Klaus. "Hindu-Christian Dialogue." The Journal of Ecumenical Studies 5:1 (1968): 21-44.

_____. "Hindu-Christian Dialogue: Its Religious and Cultural Implications." Studies in Religion 1:2 (1972):83-97.

Knitter, Paul. "What is German Protestant Theology Saying about the Non-Christian Religions?" Neue Zeitschrift für Systematische Theologie und Religionsphilosophie 15:1 (1973):38-64.

Lehmann, Paul. "The Logos in a World Come of Age." Theology Today 21:3 (1964):274-86.

Macquarrie, John. "Christianity and Other Faiths." Union Seminary Quarterly Review 20 (November 1964):39-48.

Marcus, J. T. "East and West: Phenomenologies of the Self and the Existential Bases of Knowledge." International Philosophical Quarterly 11:1 (1971):5-48.

Masson, Jacques. "Vers une rencontre du bouddhisme et du christianisme." Gregorianum 45 (1964): 306-26.

Meynell, Hugo. "Religious Disagreement." Religious Studies 9 (December 1973):427-35.

Moffitt, J. "Christianity Confronts Hinduism." _Theological Studies_ 30 (June 1969):207-24.

Neill, Stephen. "The Holy Spirit in the Non-Christian World." _Church Quarterly_ 3 (April 1971):301-11.

Niebuhr, H. Richard. "Religion and the Finality of Christ." _Harvard Divinity Bulletin_ 27 (April 1963):25-30.

Nilsson, K. O. "God, Gods and Jesus Christ." _Dialogue_ 7 (Summer 1968):178-85.

Osmond, H., and Smythies, J. "Significance of Psychotic Experience: A Reply to Prof. Zaehner." _Hibbert Journal_ 57 (April 1959):236-43.

Panikkar, Raymundo. "Category of Growth in Comparative Religion: A Critical Self-Examination." _Harvard Theological Review_ 66 (January 1973): 113-40.

_____. "Confrontation Between Hinduism and Christ." _New Blackfriars_ 50 (January 1969): 197-204.

_____. "Faith, A Constitutive Dimension of Man." _Journal of Ecumenical Studies_ 8:2 (1971): 68-81.

_____. "The Hermeneutics of Hermeneutics." _Philosophy Today_ 11 (Fall 1967):166-83.

_____. "Hinduism and Christianity." _Cross Currents_ 13 (Winter 1963):87-101.

_____. "Quelque presupposés à la rencontre des religions." _Rhythmes du Monde_ 19:1 (1971): 27-31.

_____. "Toward an Ecumenical Theandric Spirituality." _Journal of Ecumenical Studies_ 5 (Summer 1968):507-34.

Parrinder, Geoffrey. "Definitions of Mysticism." _Hibbert Journal_ 70:3 (1972):307-17.

_____. "Revelation in Other Scriptures." Studia
Missionalia 20 (1971):101-13.

Rahner, Karl. "Anonymous Christianity and the Missionary Task of the Church." I.D.O.C. 1
(4 April 1970):70-96.

Ratzinger, J. "The Changeable and the Unchangeable
in Theology." Theology Digest 10 (Spring
1962):71-76.

Sadler, A. W. "Zaehner-Huxley Debate." Journal of
Religious Thought 21:1 (1964):43-50.

Schreiner, P. "Roman Catholic Theology and Non-
Christian Religions." Journal of Ecumenical
Studies 6 (Summer 1969):376-99.

Smart, Ninian. "Anglican Contribution to the Dialogue of Religions." Theology 70 (July 1967):
302-309.

Smith, Huston. "Between Syncretism and the Ghetto."
Theology Today 20 (April 1963):21-30.

Smith, Wilfred C. "Mankind's Religiously Divided
History Approaches Self-Consciousness."
Harvard Divinity Bulletin 29 (October 1964):
1-17.

Song, C. S. "Role of Christology in the Christian
Encounter with Eastern Religions." South
East Asian Journal of Theology 5 (January
1964):13-31.

Spae, J. J. "Christ and the Religions." South East
Asian Journal of Theology 8 (January 1967):
34-52.

Staffner, H. "Conversion to Christianity Seen from
the Hindu Point of View." The Clergy Monthly
36:I (1972):3-15.

Streiker, L. D. "The Christian and the Inter-Faith
Dialogue." Journal of Religious Thought 21:2
(1964):133-44.

Takenaka, Masao. "Christian Encounter with Men of
Non-Christian Faiths in Japan." Harvard
Divinity Bulletin 27:3 (1963):11-18.

Thurian, Max. "Le dialogue avec les non-chrétiens."
    Verbum Caro 83 (1967):66-89.

Tillich, Paul; Shinn, Roger; and Lehmann, Paul. "Dis-
    cussion: Christianity and Other Faiths."
    Union Seminary Quarterly Review 20 (January
    1965):177-89.

Tong, Paul K. "Study of Thematic Differences Be-
    tween Eastern and Western Religious Thought."
    Journal of Ecumenical Studies 10 (Spring
    1973):337-60.

Book Reviews

Barclay, R. A. Review of At Sundry Times by R. C.
    Zaehner in Scottish Journal of Theology 12
    (December 1959):420-23.

Copleston, Fredrick. Review of Evolution in Religion
    by R. C. Zaehner in Heythrop Journal 12
    (October 1971):431-32.

Cunningham, Adrian. "A Third Reformation?" Review
    of Concordant Discord by R. C. Zaehner in
    New Blackfriars 54 (January 1972):8-13.

Davis, Charles. Review of Hindu and Christian in
    Vrindaban by Klaus Klostermaier in Studies
    in Religion 3:1, 81-82.

Griffiths, Bede. Review of Matter and Spirit by
    R. C. Zaehner in Blackfriars 44 (November
    1963):477-81.

Lewis, John. Review of Dialectical Christianity and
    Christian Materialism by R. C. Zaehner in
    Teilhard Review 6:2 (Winter 1971-72):106-107.

Macquarrie, John. Review of Christianity and Other
    Religions by R. C. Zaehner in Journal of
    Ecumenical Studies 2 (Fall 1965):489-90.

Mascall, Eric L. Review of Mysticism, Sacred and
    Profane by R. C. Zaehner in Church Quarterly
    Review 158 (October 1957):524-25.

161

Panikkar, Raymundo. Review of Evolution in Religion by R. C. Zaehner in Teilhard Review 6:2 (Winter 1971-72):103-104.

Smart, Ninian. Review of At Sundry Times by R. C. Zaehner in Journal of Theological Studies 11 (April 1960):239-42.

Smith, Wilfred C. Review of Concordant Discord by R. C. Zaehner in Journal of Religion 53 (July 1973):377-81.

Vollert, Cyril. Review of Matter and Spirit by R.C. Zaehner in Theological Studies 25 (March 1964):142-43.

Watkin, E. I. Review of Christianity and Other Religions by R. C. Zaehner in Downside Review 82 (October 1964):368-69.

_____. Review of Concordant Discord by R. C. Zaehner in Downside Review 89 (July 1971): 236-43.

White, Victor. Review of Foolishness to the Greeks by R. C. Zaehner in Blackfriars 35 (July-August 1954):332.

Younger, Paul. Review of Matter and Spirit by R. C. Zaehner in Theology Today 23 (October 1966): 435-39.

Zaehner, R. C. Review of Avatar and Incarnation by Geoffrey Parrinder in Theology 74 (Summer 1971):421-22.

Zinger, Donald. Review of Matter and Spirit by R. C. Zaehner in Lutheran Quarterly 17 (May 1965):171-72.